Nonfiction Writing

Grade 5

Writing: Pamela Walker
Content Editing: Leslie Sorg
James Spears
Andrea Weiss
Copy Editing: Carrie Gwynne
Art Direction: Cheryl Puckett
Cover Design: Liliana Potigian
Illustration: John Aardema
Design/Production: Carolina Caird
Susan Lovell

EMC 6015

Congratulations on your purchase of some of the finest teaching materials in the world.

Correlated to State Standards

For information about other Evan-Moor products, call 1-800-777-4362, fax 1-800-777-4332, or visit our Web site, www.evan-moor.com. Entire contents © 2011 EVAN-MOOR CORP. 18 Lower Ragsdale Drive, Monterey, CA 93940-5746. Printed in USA.

Visit *teaching-standards.com* to view a correlation of this book's activities to your state's standards. This is a free service.

CPSIA: Printed by McNaughton & Gunn, Saline, MI USA. [9/2011]

Contents

Expository Writing

Nonfiction Writing • EMC 6015 • © Evan-Moor Corp.

Persuasive Writing

Narrative Writing

How to Use This Book

Nonfiction Writing provides 16 units of instruction and practice activities. Each unit focuses on a specific nonfiction writing form and includes guided lessons with accompanying student pages that target skills essential to that writing form. The units are grouped into three sections: expository, persuasive, and narrative writing.

Teacher Pages

Use the lesson plans to provide guided instruction and modeling of the targeted skills in each unit.

A brief definition of the form offers a quick overview and simple wording to share with students.

Some lessons include an optional extension activity to further explore the skill or writing form.

The first lesson in each unit introduces key characteristics of the form and provides an opportunity to discuss and analyze a strong writing model.

The review lesson at the end of each unit guides students through the process of critiquing and revising a weak example of the writing form.

Reduced student pages provide answers and sample responses at a glance.

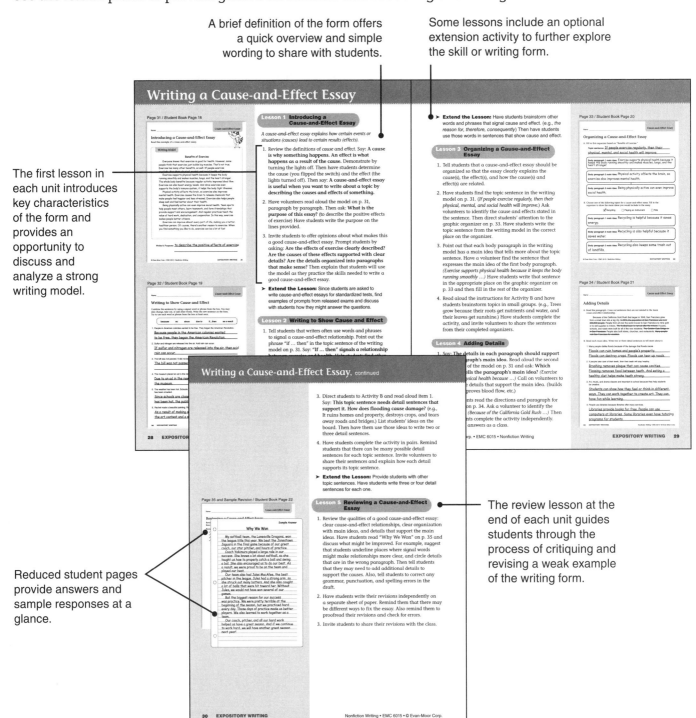

In each unit, students apply the skills they are learning by analyzing writing models and completing a variety of focused written activities.

Writing Model

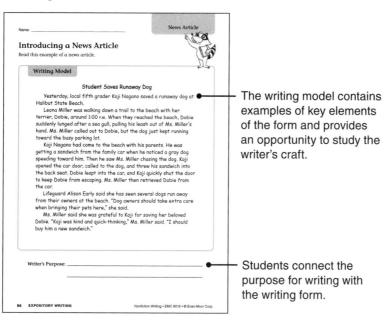

The writing model contains examples of key elements of the form and provides an opportunity to study the writer's craft.

Students connect the purpose for writing with the writing form.

Activity Pages

Students practice skills in a variety of activity formats designed to deepen their understanding of the form and craft.

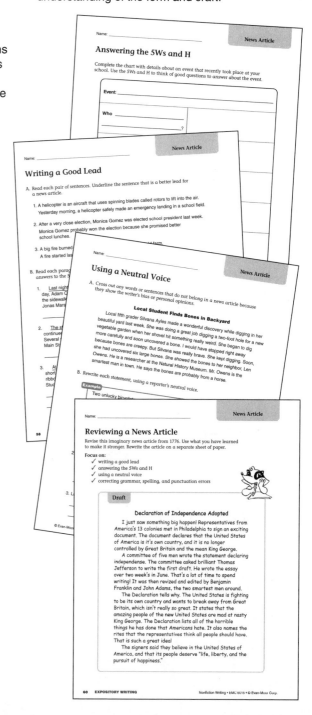

Review

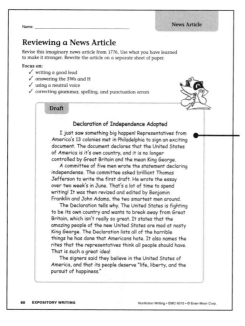

At the end of the unit, a weak model of the writing form is provided for students to revise, giving them the opportunity to review and apply all the skills they have learned.

How to Use This Book, continued

Additional Student Pages

Three of the units in this book have unique pages that are necessary to provide the appropriate modeling and support for the writing form.

Response to Literature

The first and last lessons of the *Response to Literature* unit begin with a reading selection to give students practice analyzing a writing prompt and responding to it—just as they would on a test or homework assignment.

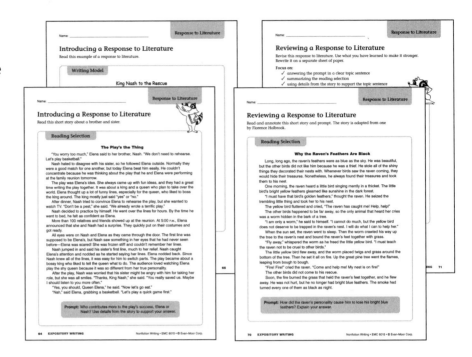

Summary

The first and last lessons of the *Summary* unit begin with a reading selection for students to summarize.

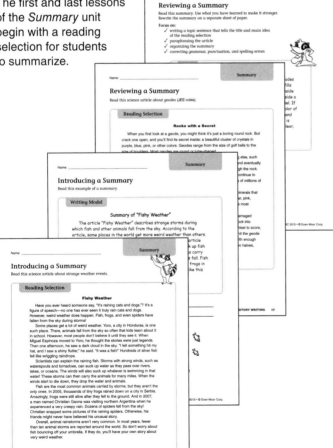

Research Report

The *Research Report* unit provides a model outline and bibliography in addition to the writing model. The review lesson of this unit asks students to revise an outline and paragraph for a report based on the information provided on the page.

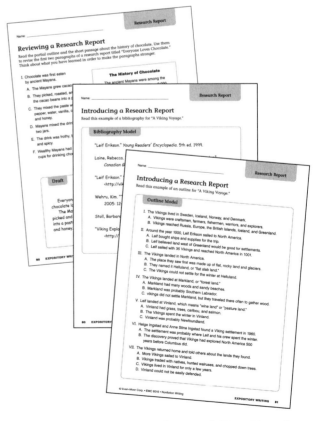

Forms of Nonfiction Writing

The following writing forms are presented in this book to provide students with a variety of real-world and academic formats and purposes for writing.

Expository Writing

Biography: a true story about a person's life, giving important information about the person and describing major events in the order in which they happened

Cause-and-Effect Essay: an essay that explains how certain events or situations (causes) lead to certain results (effects)

Compare-and-Contrast Essay: an essay that compares and contrasts two or more things, using supporting details that describe the similarities and differences

Descriptive Essay: an essay that describes a person, place, thing, or event with vivid details so the reader can easily picture it

News Article: a report that gives factual information about a current event and answers *who, what, where, when, why,* and *how* about the event

Research Report: a longer report that gives details and facts about a topic, using information gathered from different sources

Response to Literature: writing that gives a response to a prompt, or question, about a specific reading selection

Summary: a short piece of writing that gives the main idea and the most important details about a longer piece of writing, such as a story or book

Persuasive Writing

Editorial: an essay that appears in a newspaper or magazine and expresses the writer's opinions and ideas about an event or issue

Persuasive Essay: an essay written to persuade others to agree with the writer or to take a specific action

Persuasive Letter: a letter written to persuade a specific person to agree with a certain idea or to take a course of action

Problem-Solution Essay: an essay structured around the description of a specific, concrete problem and a possible solution for it

Pro-Con Essay: an essay in which a writer evaluates an idea or situation and gives his or her opinion about which side of the argument is stronger

Review: a piece of writing that gives important information and expresses an opinion about a book, movie, show, restaurant, or product

Narrative Writing

Creative Nonfiction: a true story that a writer tells, using some of the same strategies writers use when they write fiction

Personal Narrative: a true story that a writer tells about a specific event that has happened in his or her life

Writing a Summary

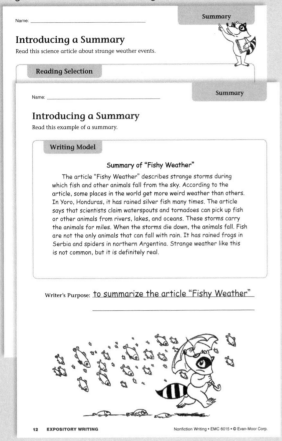

Name: _____

Summary

Introducing a Summary
Read this science article about strange weather events.

Reading Selection

Name: _____

Summary

Introducing a Summary
Read this example of a summary.

Writing Model

Summary of "Fishy Weather"

The article "Fishy Weather" describes strange storms during which fish and other animals fall from the sky. According to the article, some places in the world get more weird weather than others. In Yoro, Honduras, it has rained silver fish many times. The article says that scientists claim waterspouts and tornadoes can pick up fish or other animals from rivers, lakes, and oceans. These storms carry the animals for miles. When the storms die down, the animals fall. Fish are not the only animals that can fall with rain. It has rained frogs in Serbia and spiders in northern Argentina. Strange weather like this is not common, but it is definitely real.

Writer's Purpose: to summarize the article "Fishy Weather"

12   EXPOSITORY WRITING   Nonfiction Writing • EMC 6015 • © Evan-Moor Corp.

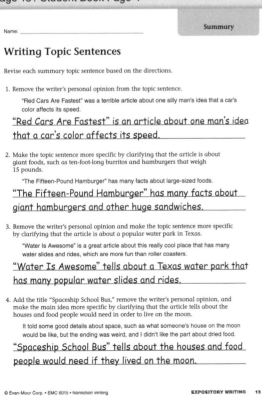

Name: _____

Summary

Writing Topic Sentences

Revise each summary topic sentence based on the directions.

1. Remove the writer's personal opinion from the topic sentence.

    "Red Cars Are Fastest" was a terrible article about one silly man's idea that a car's color affects its speed.

    "Red Cars Are Fastest" is an article about one man's idea that a car's color affects its speed.

2. Make the topic sentence more specific by clarifying that the article is about giant foods, such as ten-foot-long burritos and hamburgers that weigh 15 pounds.

    "The Fifteen-Pound Hamburger" has many facts about large-sized foods.

    "The Fifteen-Pound Hamburger" has many facts about giant hamburgers and other huge sandwiches.

3. Remove the writer's personal opinion and make the topic sentence more specific by clarifying that the article is about a popular water park in Texas.

    "Water Is Awesome" is a great article about this really cool place that has many water slides and rides, which are more fun than roller coasters.

    "Water Is Awesome" tells about a Texas water park that has many popular water slides and rides.

4. Add the title "Spaceship School Bus," remove the writer's personal opinion, and make the main idea more specific by clarifying that the article tells about the houses and food people would need in order to live on the moon.

    It told some good details about space, such as what someone's house on the moon would be like, but the ending was weird, and I didn't like the part about dried food.

    "Spaceship School Bus" tells about the houses and food people would need if they lived on the moon.

© Evan-Moor Corp. • EMC 6015 • Nonfiction Writing   EXPOSITORY WRITING   13

Lesson 1 Introducing a Summary

A summary is a short piece of writing that tells the main idea and the most important details about a longer piece of writing, such as a story, article, or book.

1. Have students recall what they did the previous night. Say: **If you had to quickly tell someone what you did last night, you would probably tell the most important or most interesting things. You would also include some details to help listeners better understand those things.** Explain that a written summary tells the most important information about a longer piece of writing, such as the main idea.

2. Have students read the article "Fishy Weather" on p. 11. Then have a volunteer read aloud the summary on p. 12. Ask: **What is the purpose of this summary?** (to summarize the article "Fishy Weather") Have students write the purpose on the lines provided.

3. Invite students to offer opinions about what makes this a good summary. Prompt students by asking: **Does one sentence tell the article's title and main idea? Does the order of the details in the summary follow the order of details in the article? Did the writer use his or her own words to tell about the article?**

Lesson 2 Writing Topic Sentences

1. Review the purpose of a summary. Say: **A good summary begins with a topic sentence that tells the title and the main idea of what is being summarized. The topic sentence should use clear language that is easy to understand. It should not include your opinions or feelings.**

2. Have students identify the topic sentence at the beginning of the model summary on p. 12. *(The article "Fishy Weather" describes strange storms during which fish and other animals fall from the sky.)* Then ask: **What is the title of the article being summarized?** ("Fishy Weather") **What is the main idea of the article?** (fish and other animals sometimes fall during storms) **Is the sentence clear and easy to understand?** (yes) **Does the summary tell the writer's thoughts or feelings?** (no)

3. Write this sentence on the board: *It tells why frogs are better pets than dogs.* Ask: **What is this topic sentence missing?** (the title of the article being summarized) Erase *It* and add the title *Frogs Rule, Dogs Drool.* Say: **This is a better topic sentence for a summary.**

4. Have students complete the activity on p. 13 independently or in small groups. Explain that there may be more than one way to revise the sentences. Invite volunteers to share their responses.

➤ **Extend the Lesson:** Assign short articles or passages from social studies textbooks to students and have them practice writing a topic sentence for a summary about that article or passage.

Lesson 3 Marking Up an Article

1. Say: **Marking up a text is a good way to find and remember information you can use in a summary of that text.**

2. Read aloud the directions for Activity A on p. 14. Then work with students to annotate "Fishy Weather." Have students draw a box around the title, double-underline the topic sentence in the introduction, and underline the main idea in each paragraph.

3. Have students complete the activities on p. 14 independently or in pairs. Then ask volunteers to share what they marked and to read aloud their responses to the question in Activity B.

➤ **Extend the Lesson:** Have students mark up a passage from a textbook or a standardized test.

Lesson 4 Paraphrasing

1. Explain that when students write a summary, they should paraphrase, or retell in their own words, ideas from an article or reading selection. Say: **When you paraphrase, you use your own words to tell the writer's ideas. You should write approximately the same amount as the text you are paraphrasing.**

2. Read aloud the third paragraph from the reading selection on p. 11. (*Scientists can explain the raining fish …*) Then challenge students to find where that information was paraphrased in the summary model on p. 12. (*scientists claim waterspouts …*) Point out that the writer kept the most important ideas from the article and that the paraphrased information is about the same length as the information from the article.

3. Direct students to the activity on p. 15 and help them paraphrase the first paragraph. Remind students that the new sentences should tell the main ideas from the paragraph. Then have students paraphrase the other two paragraphs independently or in pairs. Invite students to share their paraphrases.

Page 14 / Student Book Page 5

Name: _____   Summary

Marking Up an Article

A. Mark up this science article about onions. Do the following:
   ➤ Draw a box around the title.
   ➤ Double-underline the topic sentence in the introduction.
   ➤ Underline the main idea in each paragraph.

Why Onions Make You Cry

People have used onions to flavor their foods for thousands of years. Today, the average American eats more than 20 pounds of onions each year. But if onions are so great, why do they make people cry? The tears that you shed when you cut an onion are caused by chemicals in the onion.

Onion cells contain chemicals that sting your eyes. When you cut an onion, you cut through the walls of many onion cells. The chemicals inside those cells are released. The chemical mixes with water in your eyes and starts to sting. Your eyes start creating tears to wash away the stinging chemicals.

Cooks and scientists have come up with some ways to keep your eyes from getting bothered when you chop onions. One suggestion is to cut the onion under running water. The water will wash away the chemicals before they can reach your eyes. You can also use a fan to blow air over the onions and away from your eyes. Wearing goggles or glasses can also help by blocking the chemicals from your eyes.

If you start crying while cutting onions, don't worry. The tears will not last long, and they might even help you keep from crying the next time you start chopping. This is because each time you cut an onion, your body becomes more immune to the onion's chemicals. So dry your eyes, wash your face, and keep slicing.

B. Why do you think it is helpful to underline the main ideas in an article that you are going to summarize?

Underlining the main ideas helps me see the most important information to include in my summary.

14   EXPOSITORY WRITING   Nonfiction Writing • EMC 6015 • © Evan-Moor Corp.

Page 15 / Student Book Page 6

Name: _____   Summary

Paraphrasing

Read each paragraph. Then rewrite the information using your own words.

1. Porcupines are rodents with quills on their head, back, and sides. These quills usually lay flat. When one is disturbed, however, its quills point outward, away from its body. Each quill is sharp and can easily break off, so an animal that comes too close will end up with quills stuck in it!

   Porcupines are rodents that have sharp quills all over their bodies. Porcupines raise their quills when they are disturbed. The quills can break away from the porcupine and stick to an animal that comes too close.

2. A veterinarian named Dr. Noel Fitzpatrick found an unusual way to help animals that have lost body parts. Dr. Fitzpatrick helped a cat named Oscar that had lost its back feet in a farming accident. He made metal prosthetic feet for Oscar. These feet attach directly to Oscar's leg bones. This had never been done for an animal before.

   Dr. Noel Fitzpatrick made metal feet for a cat named Oscar. Oscar lost his feet during a farming accident. The new feet attach to Oscar's leg bones. Nobody had ever done this for an animal before.

3. The Martin Jetpack is a new jetpack that people can buy. The jetpack can travel at 60 miles per hour but can go a distance of only 35 miles. The jetpack is expected to cost $100,000. You don't need a license to fly the jetpack, but you must take a safety course before you can buy one.

   There is a jetpack now being sold called the Martin Jetpack. It can travel 35 miles at a speed of 60 miles per hour. It may cost $100,000, and people must take a safety course before they can buy the jetpack.

© Evan-Moor Corp. • EMC 6015 • Nonfiction Writing   **EXPOSITORY WRITING**   15

Page 16 / Student Book Page 7

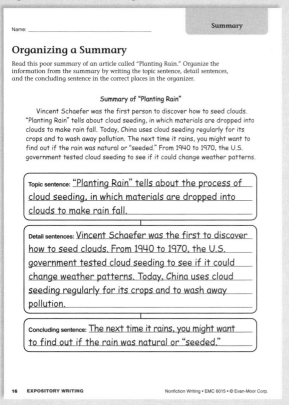

Pp. 17–18 and Sample Revision / Student Book pp. 8–9

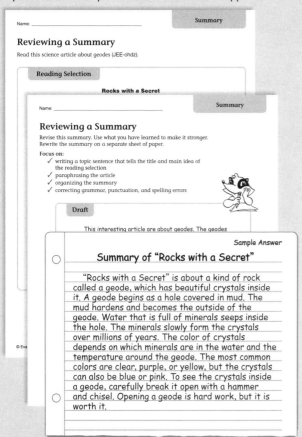

Lesson 5 Organizing a Summary

1. Review the purpose of a summary. Then say: **Summaries have three parts. The first part is the introduction, which includes the topic sentence. The second part is made up of detail sentences about the topic. The third part is a concluding sentence that wraps up the summary.**

2. On the board, draw a graphic organizer like the one on p. 16. Then have volunteers help sort sentences from the model summary on p. 12 into the organizer on the board. Point out that the detail sentences from the model flow smoothly and that their order makes sense.

3. Read aloud the directions on p. 16 and have students work in pairs to fill in the organizer. Encourage them to think about and discuss the best order for the detail sentences.

➤ **Extend the Lesson:** Have students use the graphic organizer from p. 16 to organize details for a summary of the text they used for the Lesson 3 extension activity.

Lesson 6 Reviewing a Summary

1. Review the qualities of a good summary: a clear topic sentence, correctly paraphrased information, and a clear organization.

2. Have students read and mark up "Rocks with a Secret" on p. 17 independently. Remind them to follow the steps for annotating listed on p. 14.

3. Have students read the summary on p. 18 and discuss what might be improved. For example, point out that some of the summary has been copied directly from the reading selection and not paraphrased. Also, tell students to correct any grammar, punctuation, and spelling errors in the draft.

4. Have students revise the summary independently on a separate sheet of paper. Remind them that there may be different ways to improve the summary. Also remind them to proofread their revisions and check for errors.

5. Invite volunteers to share their revisions.

Introducing a Summary

Read this science article about strange weather events.

Fishy Weather

Have you ever heard someone say, "It's raining cats and dogs"? It's a figure of speech—no one has ever seen it truly rain cats and dogs. However, weird weather does happen. Fish, frogs, and even spiders have fallen from the sky during storms!

Some places get a lot of weird weather. Yoro, a city in Honduras, is one such place. There, animals fall from the sky so often that kids learn about it in school. However, most people don't believe it until they see it. When Miguel Espinoza moved to Yoro, he thought the stories were just legends. Then one afternoon, he saw a dark cloud in the sky. "I felt something hit my hat, and I saw a shiny flutter," he said. "It was a fish!" Hundreds of silver fish fell like wriggling raindrops.

Scientists can explain the raining fish. Storms with strong winds, such as waterspouts and tornadoes, can suck up water as they pass over rivers, lakes, or oceans. The winds will also suck up whatever is swimming in that water! These storms can then carry the animals for many miles. When the winds start to die down, they drop the water and animals.

Fish are the most common animals carried by storms, but they aren't the only ones. In 2005, thousands of tiny frogs rained down on a city in Serbia. Amazingly, frogs were still alive after they fell to the ground. And in 2007, a man named Christian Gaona was visiting northern Argentina when he experienced a very creepy rain. Dozens of spiders fell from the sky! Christian snapped some pictures of the raining spiders. Otherwise, his friends might never have believed his unusual story.

Overall, animal rainstorms aren't very common. In most years, fewer than ten animal storms are reported around the world. So don't worry about fish bouncing off your umbrella. If they do, you'll have your own story about very weird weather.

Introducing a Summary

Read this example of a summary.

Writing Model

Summary of "Fishy Weather"

The article "Fishy Weather" describes strange storms during which fish and other animals fall from the sky. According to the article, some places in the world get more weird weather than others. In Yoro, Honduras, it has rained silver fish many times. The article says that scientists claim waterspouts and tornadoes can pick up fish or other animals from rivers, lakes, and oceans. These storms carry the animals for miles. When the storms die down, the animals fall. Fish are not the only animals that can fall with rain. It has rained frogs in Serbia and spiders in northern Argentina. Strange weather like this is not common, but it is definitely real.

Writer's Purpose: _____

_____

Name: _____

Writing Topic Sentences

Revise each summary topic sentence based on the directions.

1. Remove the writer's personal opinion from the topic sentence.

   "Red Cars Are Fastest" was a terrible article about one silly man's idea that a car's color affects its speed.

   _____

   _____

2. Make the topic sentence more specific by clarifying that the article is about giant foods, such as ten-foot-long burritos and hamburgers that weigh 15 pounds.

   "The Fifteen-Pound Hamburger" has many facts about large-sized foods.

   _____

   _____

3. Remove the writer's personal opinion and make the topic sentence more specific by clarifying that the article is about a popular water park in Texas.

   "Water Is Awesome" is a great article about this really cool place that has many water slides and rides, which are more fun than roller coasters.

   _____

   _____

4. Add the title "Spaceship School Bus," remove the writer's personal opinion, and make the main idea more specific by clarifying that the article tells about the houses and food people would need in order to live on the moon.

   It told some good details about space, such as what someone's house on the moon would be like, but the ending was weird, and I didn't like the part about dried food.

   _____

   _____

Name: _____

Marking Up an Article

A. Mark up this science article about onions. Do the following:
   ➤ Draw a box around the title.
   ➤ Double-underline the topic sentence in the introduction.
   ➤ Underline the main idea in each paragraph.

Why Onions Make You Cry

People have used onions to flavor their foods for thousands of years. Today, the average American eats more than 20 pounds of onions each year. But if onions are so great, why do they make people cry? The tears that you shed when you cut an onion are caused by chemicals in the onion.

Onion cells contain chemicals that sting your eyes. When you cut an onion, you cut through the walls of many onion cells. The chemicals inside those cells are released. The chemical mixes with water in your eyes and starts to sting. Your eyes start creating tears to wash away the stinging chemicals.

Cooks and scientists have come up with some ways to keep your eyes from getting bothered when you chop onions. One suggestion is to cut the onion under running water. The water will wash away the chemicals before they can reach your eyes. You can also use a fan to blow air over the onions and away from your eyes. Wearing goggles or glasses can also help by blocking the chemicals from your eyes.

If you start crying while cutting onions, don't worry. The tears will not last long, and they might even help you keep from crying the next time you start chopping. This is because each time you cut an onion, your body becomes more immune to the onion's chemicals. So dry your eyes, wash your face, and keep slicing.

B. Why do you think it is helpful to underline the main ideas in an article that you are going to summarize?

_____

_____

Paraphrasing

Read each paragraph. Then rewrite the information using your own words.

1.   Porcupines are rodents with quills on their head, back, and sides. These quills usually lay flat. When a porcupine is disturbed, however, its quills point outward, away from its body. Each quill is sharp and can easily break off, so an animal that comes too close will end up with quills stuck in it!

_____

_____

_____

_____

2.   A veterinarian named Dr. Noel Fitzpatrick found an unusual way to help animals that have lost body parts. Dr. Fitzpatrick helped a cat named Oscar that had lost its back feet in a farming accident. He made metal prosthetic feet for Oscar. These feet attach directly to Oscar's leg bones. This had never been done for an animal before.

_____

_____

_____

_____

3.   The Martin Jetpack is a new jetpack that people can buy. The jetpack can travel at 60 miles per hour but can go a distance of only 35 miles. The jetpack is expected to cost $100,000. You don't need a license to fly the jetpack, but you must take a safety course before you can buy one.

_____

_____

_____

_____

Organizing a Summary

Read this poor summary of an article called "Planting Rain." Organize the information from the summary by writing the topic sentence, detail sentences, and the concluding sentence in the correct places in the organizer.

Summary of "Planting Rain"

Vincent Schaefer was the first person to discover how to seed clouds. "Planting Rain" tells about cloud seeding, in which materials are dropped into clouds to make rain fall. Today, China uses cloud seeding regularly for its crops and to wash away pollution. The next time it rains, you might want to find out if the rain was natural or "seeded." From 1940 to 1970, the U.S. government tested cloud seeding to see if it could change weather patterns.

Topic sentence: _____

_____

_____

Detail sentences: _____

_____

_____

_____

_____

_____

Concluding sentence: _____

_____

Reviewing a Summary

Read this science article about geodes (JEE-ohdz).

Reading Selection

Rocks with a Secret

When you first look at a geode, you might think it's just a boring round rock. But crack one open, and you'll find its secret inside: a beautiful cluster of crystals in purple, blue, pink, or other colors. Geodes range from the size of golf balls to the size of boulders. Most geodes are round or tube-shaped.

A geode takes a long time to form. It begins as a hole in something else, such as a gas bubble covered in mud. The mud around the hole hardens and eventually becomes rock. Then the geode slowly fills with water that seeps through the rock. This water is full of minerals that collect and harden. As the minerals continue to seep through the geode, crystals grow on the inside. It takes hundreds of millions of years for these crystals to fully form.

The color of the crystals inside a geode depends on the kinds of minerals that seeped in and the temperature around the geode. Geodes can be clear, pink, purple, blue, or yellow inside. Clear, purple, and yellow crystals are the most common.

It takes some patience and skill to split a geode open into two undamaged halves. Simply hitting a geode with a hammer would likely break the rock into several smaller pieces. Therefore, you must first use a hammer and chisel to score, or scratch a thin line all the way around, the geode. Then you should hit the geode with the hammer and chisel in different places along the score line. With enough patience and careful hammering, the geode will eventually split into two halves, revealing its secret.

Reviewing a Summary

Revise this summary. Use what you have learned to make it stronger.
Rewrite the summary on a separate sheet of paper.

Focus on:

✓ writing a topic sentence that tells the title and main idea of
the reading selection

✓ paraphrasing the article

✓ organizing the summary

✓ correcting grammar, punctuation, and spelling errors

Draft

This interesting article are about geodes. The geodes have crystals inside them. Geodes form in mud that fills with water. This water is full of minerals that seep inside the hole to form the crystals. To see the crystals, inside a geode, break open the geode with a hammer and chisel. If your careful, you will see the beautiful secret. The color of crystals depends on which minerals are in the water and the temperature around the geode. Opening a geode is hard work, but worth it! Geode crystals are usually clear, purple, or yellow, but can also be blue or pink.

Writing a Descriptive Essay

A descriptive essay describes a person, place, thing, or event, using vivid details so that the reader can easily picture it.

1. Ask students to imagine how they would describe a favorite place to someone who had never seen it before. Explain that writing a descriptive essay, using clear and vivid details, is a good way to help readers imagine a person, place, thing, or event.

2. Have volunteers read aloud the model on p. 22, paragraph by paragraph. Ask: **What is the purpose of this essay?** (to describe Grandpa's puppet workshop) Have students write the purpose on the lines provided.

3. Remind students that a topic sentence tells what an essay is mostly about. Have students identify the topic sentence of the model. (*In his workshop, Grandpa …*)

4. Invite students to offer opinions about what makes this a good descriptive essay. Prompt students by asking: **Do the writer's descriptions help you imagine how the workshop looks, smells, and sounds? Does the writer compare things in the workshop to other things to make the description vivid?** Then explain that students will use the model as they practice the skills needed to write a good descriptive essay.

➤ **Extend the Lesson:** Have students brainstorm topics that would be good for a descriptive essay. Guide them toward concrete topics that can be described vividly. (e.g., the circus, a birthday party, a treehouse)

Lesson 2 Using Sensory Details

1. Review the purpose of a descriptive essay. Then explain that a descriptive essay has details that appeal to the five senses. Say: **Sensory details help your readers imagine that they can see, smell, hear, touch, or taste what you are describing.** Read aloud the first sentence of the third paragraph of the model on p. 22 and ask: **Which sense is the writer using to describe?** (smell) **What can you "smell"?** (wood and paint)

2. Have small groups of students underline additional sensory details in the writing model. When students have finished, ask volunteers to share what they underlined. Then ask students how those details made the workshop easier to imagine.

3. Read aloud the directions for Activity A on p. 23. Have students fill in the chart independently. Then invite volunteers to share their answers, and have other students guess what is being described.

Page 22 / Student Book Page 11

Name: _____

Descriptive Essay

Introducing a Descriptive Essay

Read this example of a descriptive essay.

Writing Model

Grandpa's Puppet Workshop

The old wooden workshop behind Grandpa's house might not look like anything special, but it is one of my favorite places to visit. In his workshop, Grandpa makes puppets for people around the world.

Jacob and Jenna are the wooden puppets guarding the workshop. They are carved to look like police officers in dark blue uniforms. Their painted eyes seem to watch you like security cameras. But, of course, they never stop visitors from entering the workshop.

The rich smell of cut wood and the strong odor of wet paint fills the air inside the workshop. Tiny pieces of sawdust slowly float in the air like lazy flies. Hard, smooth boards of strong wood lean against the workshop's back wall. Grandpa uses only the best wood to make his puppets. At one end of the workshop, Grandpa's tools are neatly arranged. Sharp saws stand in line next to heavy hammers. Pliers and screwdrivers line up like shiny silver soldiers.

Many puppets hang from the ceiling. Some are finished and ready to be sent to their new owners. Others still need faces, arms, legs, or paint. But they are all Grandpa's audience as he works on his latest creation.

Grandpa sits in the middle of the workshop on a tall stool. He wears a thick canvas apron and bends over the main worktable. A saw whines and spits as it cuts through a piece of wood. Grandpa is a happy bird as he whistles a song. Soon he will finish another puppet for another happy person.

Writer's Purpose: to describe Grandpa's puppet workshop
_____

22　EXPOSITORY WRITING　Nonfiction Writing • EMC 6015 • © Evan-Moor Corp.

Page 23 / Student Book Page 12

Name: _____

Descriptive Essay

Using Sensory Details

A. Complete the chart with sensory details that describe a sports game you have seen or been to.

I saw...	I smelled...	I heard...	I felt...	I tasted...
the lit scoreboard, players running, the shiny floor	buttery popcorn, smelly sneakers	shoes squeaking, the ball bouncing, the crowd cheering	the hard seats, the cold drink in my hands	sweet soda, cheesy pizza

B. Revise each sentence by adding sensory details. Follow the instructions given in parentheses.

Example
Music played in the dentist's waiting room. (Add details about sound.)
Slow and soothing jazz music played in the dentist's waiting room.

1. The pea soup wasn't very good. (Add details about taste.)
The pea soup was too salty.

2. My blanket is nice. (Add details about touch.)
My blanket is soft, thick, and warm.

3. The ocean looked pretty. (Add details about sight.)
The dark blue ocean was speckled with the whitecaps of waves.

4. The garbage smelled bad. (Add details about smell.)
The garbage smelled of old cheese and rotten bananas.

© Evan-Moor Corp. • EMC 6015 • Nonfiction Writing　EXPOSITORY WRITING 23

Page 24 / Student Book Page 13

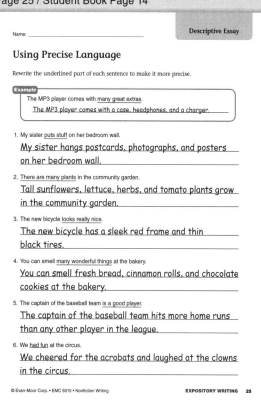

Name: _____   Descriptive Essay

Using Figurative Language

A. Underline the figurative language in each sentence. Then write whether it is a simile, a metaphor, or personification.

1. The thunder shouted at us all night long. __personification__

2. The rainstorm battered the roof like a drummer beating a drum. __simile__

3. The fog was a soft blanket covering the entire valley. __metaphor__

B. Revise each sentence so that it includes a simile, a metaphor, or personification.

Example
Bolts of lightning frequently light the night sky. **(metaphor)**
Electric eels flash in the night sky.

1. The movie was very exciting. **(metaphor)**
The movie was a roller coaster ride.

2. The car stopped very suddenly. **(personification)**
The car screamed angrily as Dad slammed on the brakes.

3. Leaves crunch under my feet. **(simile)**
Leaves crunch under my feet like cornflakes at breakfast.

4. The hurricane damaged many houses. **(metaphor)**
The hurricane was a wild animal that attacked the town.

5. The grass is long. **(personification)**
The grass reaches up to tickle my knees.

24 EXPOSITORY WRITING   Nonfiction Writing • EMC 6015 • © Evan-Moor Corp.

Page 25 / Student Book Page 14

Name: _____   Descriptive Essay

Using Precise Language

Rewrite the underlined part of each sentence to make it more precise.

Example
The MP3 player comes with many great extras.
The MP3 player comes with a case, headphones, and a charger.

1. My sister puts stuff on her bedroom wall.
My sister hangs postcards, photographs, and posters on her bedroom wall.

2. There are many plants in the community garden.
Tall sunflowers, lettuce, herbs, and tomato plants grow in the community garden.

3. The new bicycle looks really nice.
The new bicycle has a sleek red frame and thin black tires.

4. You can smell many wonderful things at the bakery.
You can smell fresh bread, cinnamon rolls, and chocolate cookies at the bakery.

5. The captain of the baseball team is a good player.
The captain of the baseball team hits more home runs than any other player in the league.

6. We had fun at the circus.
We cheered for the acrobats and laughed at the clowns in the circus.

© Evan-Moor Corp. • EMC 6015 • Nonfiction Writing   EXPOSITORY WRITING 25

4. Direct students to the example in Activity B. Say: **The revised sentence tells us how the music sounded in the waiting room. It gives us clear details so we can better imagine what the music sounds like.**

5. Have students complete Activity B independently or in pairs. Then have students read aloud their revisions.

Lesson 3 Using Figurative Language

1. Remind students that a good descriptive essay helps a reader imagine the topic. Say: **Writers often describe things by using figurative language such as *similes*, *metaphors*, and *personification*. Similes and metaphors compare things to make an interesting image or connection. A simile compares things using *like* or *as*.** (e.g., The evening clouds looked like pink cotton candy.) **A metaphor compares things without using *like* or *as*.** (e.g., The river was a blue ribbon winding down the mountain.) **Personification gives human traits or actions to an animal or an object.** (e.g., The tree danced in the wind.)

2. Help students identify examples of each type of figurative language in the writing model on p. 22. (simile: like security cameras, like lazy flies, like shiny silver soldiers; personification: saws stand in line; metaphor: Grandpa is a happy bird)

3. Have students complete Activity A on p. 24 in pairs. Ask students to identify what is being personified and what is compared in the simile and metaphor. (1. thunder, 2. rain and drummer, 3. fog and blanket)

4. Read aloud the directions for Activity B and discuss the example. Then have students complete the activity independently or in pairs. Remind students that there are many ways to revise the sentences. Then invite volunteers to share their revisions.

Lesson 4 Using Precise Language

1. Remind students that the purpose of a descriptive essay is to describe something so that a reader can imagine it. Then say: **Good writers use specific, descriptive words instead of vague or general words.** On the board, write: *Grandpa has many tools there.* Then challenge students to find the more precise revision of that sentence in the writing model on p. 22. (*At one end of the workshop, Grandpa's tools …*) Ask: **How does the more precise sentence create a clearer picture that is easier to imagine?** (e.g., The sentence tells where the tools are and what kind of order they're in.)

2. Direct students to p. 25. Ask a volunteer to read the example aloud. Say: **The phrase "many great extras" is vague. Why is the revision more clear and precise?** (It tells what the extras are and helps readers form a clearer picture.)

3. Have students complete the activity independently. Then invite volunteers to share their revisions and tell how using precise language improved the sentences.

Lesson 5   Avoiding Overwriting

1. Review the purpose of a descriptive essay. Then say: **Sometimes it's easy to get caught up in writing details, being precise, and using figurative language. Too much of this writing can distract and confuse readers. Be careful not to overwrite, or use too many words and details to describe things.**

2. Read aloud the directions on p. 26 and discuss the example. Say: **The first sentence has so many words and details to describe the saw that I don't know what to focus on. It's confusing.** Then read the revision aloud and ask students to recall where they've read that sentence before. Say: **This is the sentence that ended up in "Grandpa's Puppet Workshop." It gives a clear picture of the saw and what it is doing, but the sentence uses fewer words. It is easier to understand, and it is still descriptive.**

3. Complete the first two items on p. 26 with students. Have them identify what is wrong with each sentence and suggest ways to fix it. Then have students complete the activity independently or in pairs. Invite volunteers to share their new sentences and explain why their revisions are better.

Lesson 6   Reviewing a Descriptive Essay

1. Review the qualities of a good descriptive essay: sensory details, figurative language, precise language, and no overwriting. Then have students read "Kitchen at Six" on p. 27 and discuss how they might improve it. For example, brainstorm types of bakery food and the smells and sounds students have encountered at a bakery or at home when someone baked a treat. Also, tell students to correct any grammar, punctuation, and spelling errors in the draft.

2. Have students revise the essay independently on a separate sheet of paper. Remind them that there may be different ways to fix the descriptive essay.

Page 26 / Student Book Page 15

Name: _____   Descriptive Essay

Avoiding Overwriting

Revise each sentence by removing excessive detail, unnecessary figurative language, and repetitive words and phrases.

Example
A heavy yellow saw whines and spits and squeals as it carefully and slowly cuts a three-foot-long piece of wood.
A saw whines and spits as it cuts through a piece of wood.

1. Adele stroked the little, teeny, tiny, small baby kitten.
Adele stroked the tiny baby kitten.

2. Meli thought her food was as cold as ice in a freezer at the North Pole during winter.
Meli thought her food was as cold as ice.

3. Mr. Cruz lent us his brand-new lawnmower that cost $90 that he bought on sale at the hardware store because his old one died three weeks ago.
Mr. Cruz lent us his new lawnmower.

4. My new remote-control car is so fast that it zooms, flies, and speeds around the track.
My new remote-control car zooms around the track.

5. The chicken combo includes two pieces of chicken, mashed potatoes with gravy, green beans, a fork, a spoon, two napkins, and a tray that holds everything.
The chicken combo includes two pieces of chicken, mashed potatoes with gravy, and green beans.

6. The loudspeaker squawked like a chicken and screeched like a hawk and hummed like a hummingbird as Principal Bruce read the morning announcements.
The loudspeaker squawked like a chicken as Principal Bruce read the morning announcements.

26   EXPOSITORY WRITING   Nonfiction Writing • EMC 6015 • © Evan-Moor Corp.

Page 27 and Sample Revision / Student Book Page 16

Name: _____   Descriptive Essay

Sample Answer

Kitchen at Six

Clark's Bakery is a great place to eat. Clark, the baker, makes yummy breads, muffins, and cookies. At six in the morning, people crowd into the bakery. They shout orders and smile happily.

The kitchen is as hot as a sauna. Clark and his two assistants make batter, fill pans, and move food in and out of the ovens. Stacks of trays and pans sit patiently on the table in the back, waiting to be used. Giant mounds of bread dough expand like fluffy clouds in large glass bowls. Three enormous mixers work constantly. Timers remind Clark to check the oven.

The bakery shelves are in the front of the store. Different breads, muffins, and rolls wait eagerly to be eaten. A beautiful pastry shines like a new penny.

The best part of visiting Clark's Bakery is choosing a special treat for breakfast. His muffins and pastries make the morning yummy!

Name: _____

Introducing a Descriptive Essay

Read this example of a descriptive essay.

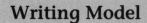

Writing Model

Grandpa's Puppet Workshop

The old wooden workshop behind Grandpa's house might not look like anything special, but it is one of my favorite places to visit. In his workshop, Grandpa makes puppets for people around the world.

Jacob and Jenna are the wooden puppets guarding the workshop. They are carved to look like police officers in dark blue uniforms. Their painted eyes seem to watch you like security cameras. But, of course, they never stop visitors from entering the workshop.

The rich smell of cut wood and the strong odor of wet paint fills the air inside the workshop. Tiny pieces of sawdust slowly float in the air like lazy flies. Hard, smooth boards of strong wood lean against the workshop's back wall. Grandpa uses only the best wood to make his puppets. At one end of the workshop, Grandpa's tools are neatly arranged. Sharp saws stand in line next to heavy hammers. Pliers and screwdrivers line up like shiny silver soldiers.

Many puppets hang from the ceiling. Some are finished and ready to be sent to their new owners. Others still need faces, arms, legs, or paint. But they are all Grandpa's audience as he works on his latest creation.

Grandpa sits in the middle of the workshop on a tall stool. He wears a thick canvas apron and bends over the main worktable. A saw whines and spits as it cuts through a piece of wood. Grandpa is a happy bird as he whistles a song. Soon he will finish another puppet for another happy person.

Writer's Purpose: _____

_____

Using Sensory Details

A. Complete the chart with sensory details that describe a sports game you have seen or been to.

I saw...	I smelled...	I heard...	I felt...	I tasted...

B. Revise each sentence by adding sensory details. Follow the instructions given in parentheses.

Example

Music played in the dentist's waiting room. (Add details about sound.)

Slow and soothing jazz music played in the dentist's waiting room.

1. The pea soup wasn't very good. (Add details about taste.)

   _____

2. My blanket is nice. (Add details about touch.)

   _____

3. The ocean looked pretty. (Add details about sight.)

   _____

4. The garbage smelled bad. (Add details about smell.)

   _____

Name: _____

Using Figurative Language

A. Underline the figurative language in each sentence. Then write whether it is a simile, a metaphor, or personification.

1. The thunder shouted at us all night long. _____

2. The rainstorm battered the roof like a drummer beating a drum. _____

3. The fog was a soft blanket covering the entire valley. _____

B. Revise each sentence so that it includes a simile, a metaphor, or personification.

> **Example**
>
> Bolts of lightning frequently light the night sky. **(metaphor)**
>
> <u>Electric eels flash in the night sky.</u>

1. The movie was very exciting. **(metaphor)**

   _____

2. The car stopped very suddenly. **(personification)**

   _____

3. Leaves crunch under my feet. **(simile)**

   _____

4. The hurricane damaged many houses. **(metaphor)**

   _____

5. The grass is long. **(personification)**

   _____

Using Precise Language

Rewrite the underlined part of each sentence to make it more precise.

> **Example**
>
> The MP3 player comes with <u>many great extras</u>.
>
> <u>The MP3 player comes with a case, headphones, and a charger.</u>

1. My sister <u>puts stuff</u> on her bedroom wall.

   _____

   _____

2. <u>There are many plants</u> in the community garden.

   _____

   _____

3. The new bicycle <u>looks really nice</u>.

   _____

   _____

4. You can smell <u>many wonderful things</u> at the bakery.

   _____

   _____

5. The captain of the baseball team <u>is a good player</u>.

   _____

   _____

6. We <u>had fun</u> at the circus.

   _____

   _____

Avoiding Overwriting

Revise each sentence by removing excessive detail, unnecessary figurative language, and repetitive words and phrases.

> **Example**
>
> A heavy yellow saw whines and spits and squeals as it carefully and slowly cuts a three-foot-long piece of wood.
>
> _A saw whines and spits as it cuts through a piece of wood._

1. Adele stroked the little, teeny, tiny, small baby kitten.

   _____

2. Meli thought her food was as cold as ice in a freezer at the North Pole during winter.

   _____

3. Mr. Cruz lent us his brand-new lawnmower that cost $90 that he bought on sale at the hardware store because his old one died three weeks ago.

   _____

4. My new remote-control car is so fast that it zooms, flies, and speeds around the track.

   _____

5. The chicken combo includes two pieces of chicken, mashed potatoes with gravy, green beans, a fork, a spoon, two napkins, and a tray that holds everything.

   _____

   _____

6. The loudspeaker squawked like a chicken and screeched like a hawk and hummed like a hummingbird as Principal Bruce read the morning announcements.

   _____

   _____

Reviewing a Descriptive Essay

Revise this descriptive essay. Use what you have learned to make it stronger. Rewrite the essay on a separate sheet of paper.

Focus on:
- ✓ including sensory details, similes, metaphors, and personification so that readers can imagine the topic
- ✓ using precise words to describe
- ✓ avoiding overwriting
- ✓ correcting grammar, punctuation, and spelling errors

Draft

Kitchen at Six

Clark's Bakery is a place to eat. Clark, the baker, makes yummy foods At six in the morning, there's a lot going on.

The kitchen is always hot. There are sevrull ovens. Clark and his assistants run around and do stuff. Pans and trays are on a table. Cookie doe is in bowls Three giant white and silver loud mixers are blending and swirling and whipping and whisking and kneading and churning and turning. Timers are beeping. Like reminders.

In the front of the bakery are the cash rejister and the display shelves. There are all kinds of good things to eat on the shelves. Everything looks and smells really good.

The best part of visiting Clark's Bakery, is choosing a special treat for breakfast. His food makes the morning yummy!

Writing a Cause-and-Effect Essay

Name: _____

Cause-and-Effect Essay

Introducing a Cause-and-Effect Essay

Read this example of a cause-and-effect essay.

Writing Model

Benefits of Exercise

Everyone knows that exercise is good for health. However, some people think that exercise just builds big muscles. That's not true. Exercise has many other benefits, as well. If people exercise regularly, then their physical, mental, and social health will improve.

Exercise supports physical health because it keeps the body running smoothly and makes muscles, lungs, and the heart stronger. The whole body benefits because regular activity improves blood flow. Exercise can also boost energy levels. And since exercise even supports the body's immune system, it helps the body fight illnesses.

Physical activity affects the brain, so exercise also improves mental health. Exercise causes the brain to release chemicals that make people feel happier and less stressed. Exercise also helps people sleep well and feel better about their health.

Being physically active can even improve social health. Team sports help people meet others, learn teamwork, and form friendships that provide support and encouragement. And regular practices teach the value of hard work, dedication, and cooperation. In this way, exercise makes people better citizens.

Exercise can improve almost every part of life, making you a better, healthier person. Of course, there's another reason to exercise. When you find something you like to do, exercise can be a lot of fun!

Writer's Purpose: to describe the positive effects of exercise
_____

© Evan-Moor Corp. • EMC 6015 • Nonfiction Writing   EXPOSITORY WRITING   **31**

Name: _____

Cause-and-Effect Essay

Writing to Show Cause and Effect

Combine the sentences by using a signal word or phrase from the box. You may also change, take out, or add other words. Write the new sentence on the lines. Try to use each word or phrase from the box at least once.

because	so	since	due to	if...then	as a result

1. People in American colonies wanted to be free. They began the American Revolution.

   Because people in the American colonies wanted to be free, they began the American Revolution.

2. Sulfur and nitrogen are released into the air. Acid rain can occur.

   If sulfur and nitrogen are released into the air, then acid rain can occur.

3. The bill was not passed. It did not become state law.

   The bill was not passed, so it did not become state law.

4. The museum placed an ad in the newspaper. More people came to the museum.

   Due to an ad in the newspaper, more people came to the museum.

5. The weather has been hot. Schools are closed for the summer. The public pool has been crowded.

   Since schools are closed for the summer and the weather has been hot, the public pool has been crowded.

6. Rachel made a beautiful painting. Rachel won the art contest. She won a scholarship.

   As a result of making a beautiful painting, Rachel won the art contest and a scholarship.

32   EXPOSITORY WRITING   Nonfiction Writing • EMC 6015 • © Evan-Moor Corp.

Lesson 1 Introducing a Cause-and-Effect Essay

A cause-and-effect essay explains how certain events or situations (causes) lead to certain results (effects).

1. Review the definitions of *cause* and *effect*. Say: **A cause is why something happens. An effect is what happens as a result of the cause.** Demonstrate by turning the lights off. Then have students determine the cause (you flipped the switch) and the effect (the lights turned off). Then say: **A cause-and-effect essay is useful when you want to write about a topic by describing the causes and effects of something.**

2. Have volunteers read aloud the model on p. 31, paragraph by paragraph. Then ask: **What is the purpose of this essay?** (to describe the positive effects of exercise) Have students write the purpose on the lines provided.

3. Invite students to offer opinions about what makes this a good cause-and-effect essay. Prompt students by asking: **Are the effects of exercise clearly described? Are the causes of these effects supported with clear details? Are the details organized into paragraphs that make sense?** Then explain that students will use the model as they practice the skills needed to write a good cause-and-effect essay.

➤ **Extend the Lesson:** Since students are asked to write cause-and-effect essays for standardized tests, find examples of prompts from released exams and discuss with students how they might answer the questions.

Lesson 2 Writing to Show Cause and Effect

1. Tell students that writers often use words and phrases to signal a cause-and-effect relationship. Point out the phrase "if … then" in the topic sentence of the writing model on p. 31. Say: **"If … then" signals a relationship between exercise and health.** Help students find other signal words in the model and have them identify the relationships that the words signal. (*because*, exercise and physical health; *so*, exercise and mental health; *in this way*, exercise and being better citizens)

2. Direct students to p. 32. Read the instructions aloud and draw students' attention to the last two items on the page. Say: **Sometimes a cause can have more than one effect and an effect can have more than one cause.** If needed, model how to write a sentence that describes multiple causes or effects. Then have students complete the activity.

➤ **Extend the Lesson:** Have students brainstorm other words and phrases that signal cause and effect. (e.g., *the reason for, therefore, consequently*) Then have students use those words in sentences that show cause and effect.

Lesson 3 Organizing a Cause-and-Effect Essay

1. Tell students that a cause-and-effect essay should be organized so that the essay clearly explains the cause(s), the effect(s), and how the cause(s) and effect(s) are related.

2. Have students find the topic sentence in the writing model on p. 31. (*If people exercise regularly, then their physical, mental, and social health will improve.*) Ask volunteers to identify the cause and effects stated in the sentence. Then direct students' attention to the graphic organizer on p. 33. Have students write the topic sentence from the writing model in the correct place on the organizer.

3. Point out that each body paragraph in the writing model has a main idea that tells more about the topic sentence. Have a volunteer find the sentence that expresses the main idea of the first body paragraph. (*Exercise supports physical health because it keeps the body running smoothly …*) Have students write that sentence in the appropriate place on the graphic organizer on p. 33 and then fill in the rest of the organizer.

4. Read aloud the instructions for Activity B and have students brainstorm topics in small groups. (e.g., Trees grow because their roots get nutrients and water, and their leaves get sunshine.) Have students complete the activity, and invite volunteers to share the sentences from their completed organizers.

Lesson 4 Adding Details

1. Say: **The details in each paragraph should support that paragraph's main idea.** Read aloud the second paragraph of the model on p. 31 and ask: **Which sentence tells the paragraph's main idea?** (*Exercise supports physical health because …*) Call on volunteers to identify the details that support the main idea. (builds muscle, improves blood flow, etc.)

2. Have students read the directions and paragraph for Activity A on p. 34. Ask a volunteer to identify the main idea. (*Because of the California Gold Rush …*) Then have students complete the activity independently. Review the answers as a class.

Page 33 / Student Book Page 20

Name: _____

Cause-and-Effect Essay

Organizing a Cause-and-Effect Essay

A. Fill in this organizer based on "Benefits of Exercise."

Topic sentence: If people exercise regularly, then their physical, mental, and social health will improve.

Body paragraph 1 main idea: Exercise supports physical health because it keeps the body running smoothly and makes muscles, lungs, and the heart stronger.

Body paragraph 2 main idea: Physical activity affects the brain, so exercise also improves mental health.

Body paragraph 3 main idea: Being physically active can even improve social health.

B. Choose one of the following topics for a cause-and-effect essay. Fill in the organizer to show the main ideas you would include in the essay.

☑ Recycling   ☐ Playing an Instrument   ☐ Pets

Body paragraph 1 main idea: Recycling is helpful because it saves energy.

Body paragraph 2 main idea: Recycling is also helpful because it saves water.

Body paragraph 3 main idea: Recycling also keeps some trash out of landfills.

© Evan-Moor Corp. • EMC 6015 • Nonfiction Writing   EXPOSITORY WRITING   33

Page 34 / Student Book Page 21

Name: _____

Cause-and-Effect Essay

Adding Details

A. Read the paragraph. Cross out sentences that are not related to the main cause-and-effect relationship.

Because of the California Gold Rush that began in 1848, San Francisco grew from a small town into a big city. ~~In 2010, the population of San Francisco was over 800,000 people.~~ People from all over the world moved to San Francisco to mine gold or to sell supplies to miners. ~~The football team is named after the miners.~~ Houses, schools, and roads were built for all of the new residents. ~~The Golden Gate Bridge is in San Francisco.~~ People also built stores, churches, and restaurants. ~~Many people visit San Francisco for vacation.~~

B. Read each main idea. Write two or three detail sentences to tell more about it.

1. Many people dislike floods because of the damage that floods cause.
   Floods can ruin homes and people's property. Floods can destroy crops. Floods can tear up roads.

2. If people take care of their teeth, then their teeth will stay healthy.
   Brushing removes plaque that can cause cavities. Flossing removes food between teeth. And eating a healthy diet helps make teeth strong.

3. Art, music, and drama classes are important in school because they help students be creative.
   Students can show how they feel or think in different ways. They can work together to create art. They can have fun while learning.

4. People use libraries because libraries offer many services.
   Libraries provide books for free. People can use computers at libraries. Some libraries even have tutoring programs for students.

34   EXPOSITORY WRITING   Nonfiction Writing • EMC 6015 • © Evan-Moor Corp.

3. Direct students to Activity B and read aloud item 1. Say: **This topic sentence needs detail sentences that support it. How does flooding cause damage?** (e.g., It ruins homes and property, destroys crops, and tears away roads and bridges.) List students' ideas on the board. Then have them use those ideas to write two or three detail sentences.

4. Have students complete the activity in pairs. Remind students that there can be many possible detail sentences for each topic sentence. Invite volunteers to share their sentences and explain how each detail supports its topic sentence.

➤ **Extend the Lesson:** Provide students with other topic sentences. Have students write three or four detail sentences for each one.

Lesson 5 Reviewing a Cause-and-Effect Essay

1. Review the qualities of a good cause-and-effect essay: clear cause-and-effect relationships, clear organization with main ideas, and details that support the main ideas. Have students read "Why We Won" on p. 35 and discuss what might be improved. For example, suggest that students underline places where signal words might make relationships more clear, and circle details that are in the wrong paragraph. Then tell students that they may need to add additional details to support the causes. Also, tell students to correct any grammar, punctuation, and spelling errors in the draft.

2. Have students write their revisions independently on a separate sheet of paper. Remind them that there may be different ways to fix the essay. Also remind them to proofread their revisions and check for errors.

3. Invite students to share their revisions with the class.

Page 35 and Sample Revision / Student Book Page 22

Name: _____

Cause-and-Effect Essay

Reviewing a Cause-and-Effect Essay

Revis
Rewr

Focu

Sample Answer

Why We Won

My softball team, the Lanesville Dragons, won the league title this year. We beat the Jonestown Jaguars in the final game because of our great coach, our star pitcher, and hours of practice.

Coach Yakimura played a large role in our success. She knows a lot about softball, so she taught us how to properly catch a ball and swing a bat. She also encouraged us to do our best. As a result, we were proud to be on the team and played our best.

Our team also had Jules MacAfee, the best pitcher in the league. Jules had a strong arm, so she struck out many batters. And she also caught a lot of balls that were hit toward her. Without Jules, we would not have won several of our games.

But the biggest reason for our success was practice. We were pretty terrible at the beginning of the season, but we practiced hard every day. Those days of practice made us better players. We also learned to work together as a team.

Our coach, pitcher, and all our hard work helped us have a great season. And if we continue to work hard, we will have another great season next year!

Name: _____

Introducing a Cause-and-Effect Essay

Read this example of a cause-and-effect essay.

Writing Model

Benefits of Exercise

Everyone knows that exercise is good for health. However, some people think that exercise just builds big muscles. That's not true. Exercise has many other benefits, as well. If people exercise regularly, then their physical, mental, and social health will improve.

Exercise supports physical health because it keeps the body running smoothly and makes muscles, lungs, and the heart stronger. The whole body benefits because regular activity improves blood flow. Exercise can also boost energy levels. And since exercise even supports the body's immune system, it helps the body fight illnesses.

Physical activity affects the brain, so exercise also improves mental health. Exercise causes the brain to release chemicals that make people feel happier and less stressed. Exercise also helps people sleep well and feel better about their health.

Being physically active can even improve social health. Team sports help people meet others, learn teamwork, and form friendships that provide support and encouragement. And regular practices teach the value of hard work, dedication, and cooperation. In this way, exercise makes people better citizens.

Exercise can improve almost every part of life, making you a better, healthier person. Of course, there's another reason to exercise. When you find something you like to do, exercise can be a lot of fun!

Writer's Purpose: _____

_____

Writing to Show Cause and Effect

Combine the sentences by using a signal word or phrase from the box. You may also change, take out, or add other words. Write the new sentence on the lines. Try to use each word or phrase from the box at least once.

because	so	since	due to	if...then	as a result

1. People in American colonies wanted to be free. They began the American Revolution.

   _____

   _____

2. Sulfur and nitrogen are released into the air. Acid rain can occur.

   _____

   _____

3. The bill was not passed. It did not become state law.

   _____

   _____

4. The museum placed an ad in the newspaper. More people came to the museum.

   _____

   _____

5. The weather has been hot. Schools are closed for the summer. The public pool has been crowded.

   _____

   _____

6. Rachel made a beautiful painting. Rachel won the art contest. She won a scholarship.

   _____

   _____

Nonfiction Writing • EMC 6015 • © Evan-Moor Corp.

Organizing a Cause-and-Effect Essay

A. Fill in this organizer based on "Benefits of Exercise."

Topic sentence: _____

_____

Body paragraph 1 main idea:

Body paragraph 2 main idea:

Body paragraph 3 main idea:

B. Choose one of the following topics for a cause-and-effect essay. Fill in the organizer to show the main ideas you would include in the essay.

☐ Recycling ☐ Playing an Instrument ☐ Pets

Body paragraph 1 main idea:

Body paragraph 2 main idea:

Body paragraph 3 main idea:

Adding Details

A. Read the paragraph. Cross out sentences that are not related to the main cause-and-effect relationship.

> Because of the California Gold Rush that began in 1848, San Francisco grew from a small town into a big city. In 2010, the population of San Francisco was over 800,000 people. People from all over the world moved to San Francisco to mine gold or to sell supplies to miners. The football team is named after the miners. Houses, schools, and roads were built for all of the new residents. The Golden Gate Bridge is in San Francisco. People also built stores, churches, and restaurants. Many people visit San Francisco for vacation.

B. Read each main idea. Write two or three detail sentences to tell more about it.

1. Many people dislike floods because of the damage that floods cause.

   _____

   _____

2. If people take care of their teeth, then their teeth will stay healthy.

   _____

   _____

   _____

3. Art, music, and drama classes are important in school because they help students be creative.

   _____

   _____

   _____

4. People use libraries because libraries offer many services.

   _____

   _____

   _____

Reviewing a Cause-and-Effect Essay

Revise this cause-and-effect essay. Use what you have learned to make it stronger.
Rewrite the essay on a separate sheet of paper.

Focus on:

✓ using signal words and phrases to show cause and effect
✓ organizing causes and effects with main-idea sentences
✓ adding details that support each main-idea sentence
✓ correcting grammar, punctuation, and spelling errors

Draft

Why We Won

My softball team, the Lanesville Dragons, won the leeg title this year. We beat the Jonestown Jaguars in the final game. We had a great coach. Our pitcher was a star. We practissed for hours.

Coach Yakimura played a large role in our succeed. She knew a lot about softball. She taught us how, to properly catch a ball and swing a bat. Without Jules, we would not have one our games. As a result, we were proud to be on the team, and we played our best.

Our team had Jules MacAfee, the best pitcher in the league. We was pretty terrible at the beginning of the season, but we to practiss hard every day. Jules had a strong arm, so she struck out many batters. She also caught a lot of balls. That were hit to her.

But the biggest reason for our success was practiss. Those days of practiss made us better players. We also learned to work together better. Coach Yakimura encouraged us to do our best.

We had a coach and a pitcher, and we worked hard. These things helped us to have a great season. If we keep working hard, our next season will be better!

Writing a Compare-and-Contrast Essay

Page 39 / Student Book Page 24

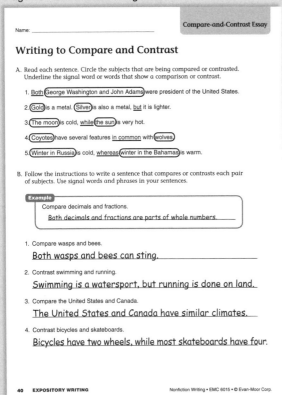

Name: _____

Compare-and-Contrast Essay

Introducing a Compare-and-Contrast Essay

Read this example of a compare-and-contrast essay.

Writing Model

What's Playing Tonight?

If you want to see people act out a story, you can go to a movie or a play. Movies and plays have many things in common, but there are some big differences between them, as well.

Movies and plays are both forms of entertainment in which people act out stories. In both cases, actors memorize a script and pretend to be different characters. Movies and plays also have directors who tell the actors where to stand and how to say their lines. In addition, both movies and plays can be funny, sad, exciting, or even a little boring at times.

However, there are many differences between plays and movies. First of all, plays have been around for thousands of years, but movies have been around for only a hundred years or so. Plays are performed live, whereas movies are filmed with cameras and shown to audiences later. Audiences must go to a theater or another special place to see a play. However, people can watch a movie almost anywhere, such as in a theater, in a living room, or even sitting in front of a computer. Another difference is that movies often have more special effects than plays do. And movies can be filmed in many places, which means that the settings can change more often in movies than in plays.

Movies and plays can be equally wonderful, and one isn't better than the other. It just depends on what you feel like seeing. Are you in the mood for the excitement of a live performance, or the special effects and convenience of a movie? Thinking about how movies and plays are alike and different can help you decide what kind of show you want to see.

Writer's Purpose: _to compare and contrast movies and plays_

_____

© Evan-Moor Corp. • EMC 6015 • Nonfiction Writing   **EXPOSITORY WRITING   39**

Page 40 / Student Book Page 25

Name: _____

Compare-and-Contrast Essay

Writing to Compare and Contrast

A. Read each sentence. Circle the subjects that are being compared or contrasted. Underline the signal word or words that show a comparison or contrast.

1. Both (George Washington and John Adams) were president of the United States.
2. (Gold) is a metal. (Silver) is also a metal, but it is lighter.
3. (The moon) is cold, while (the sun) is very hot.
4. (Coyotes) have several features in common with (wolves).
5. (Winter in Russia) is cold, whereas (winter in the Bahamas) is warm.

B. Follow the instructions to write a sentence that compares or contrasts each pair of subjects. Use signal words and phrases in your sentences.

Example

Compare decimals and fractions.
Both decimals and fractions are parts of whole numbers.

1. Compare wasps and bees.
Both wasps and bees can sting.

2. Contrast swimming and running.
Swimming is a watersport, but running is done on land.

3. Compare the United States and Canada.
The United States and Canada have similar climates.

4. Contrast bicycles and skateboards.
Bicycles have two wheels, while most skateboards have four.

40   EXPOSITORY WRITING   Nonfiction Writing • EMC 6015 • © Evan-Moor Corp.

A compare-and-contrast essay is writing that makes a comparison between two or more things, using supporting details to describe the similarities and differences.

1. Explain to students that when they want to describe the similarities and differences between two things, places, events, or ideas, they can write a compare-and-contrast essay. If necessary, remind students that _comparing_ means describing the similarities between two or more things, and _contrasting_ means describing the differences.

2. Have students read the model on p. 39. Then ask: **What is the purpose of this essay?** (to compare and contrast movies and plays) Have students write the purpose on the lines provided.

3. Invite students to offer opinions about what makes this a good compare-and-contrast essay. Prompt students by asking: **Does the first paragraph make clear which two things are being compared or contrasted? Are the details organized in a way that makes sense? Is there enough information about both subjects? Does the last paragraph let you know that the essay is ending?** Then explain that students will use the model as they practice the skills needed to write a good compare-and-contrast essay.

Lesson 2 Writing to Compare and Contrast

1. Review the purpose of a compare-and-contrast essay. Say: **When you write to compare and contrast, your sentences should state the main idea and contain words to signal whether you are comparing or contrasting subjects.** Write this sentence from "What's Playing Tonight?" on the board: _Plays have been around for thousands of years, but movies have been around for only a hundred years or so._ Ask: **What are the two subjects of this sentence?** (plays and movies) **Are they being compared or contrasted?** (contrasted) **How do you know?** (because of the signal word _but_) Explain: **Signal words and phrases tell your readers whether you are comparing or contrasting.**

2. As a class, brainstorm other words or phrases that signal comparison (e.g., _same, alike, in common_) and contrast (_though, however, but, while_). List the words on the board. Then have students circle signal words and phrases in "What's Playing Tonight?" (_in common, differences, both, however, but, whereas, equally, alike, different,_ etc.)

3. Direct students to p. 40 and read the instructions for Activity A aloud. Have students complete the activity. Then check the answers as a class.

4. Read aloud the instructions for Activity B and discuss the example with students. Then have them complete the activity. Remind students to use signal words and phrases listed on the board.

Lesson 3 Organizing Details

1. Review the purpose of a compare-and-contrast essay. Say: **An essay should be clearly organized so that the reader can easily follow the writer's ideas.**

2. Explain: **The details in a compare-and-contrast essay can be organized in different ways. For example, each paragraph can have details about one of the subjects being compared. You can also organize details into a paragraph that focuses on the similarities between subjects and one that focuses on the differences. No type of organization is better than the other, so choose the type you think fits your essay best.**

3. Ask students which form of organization "What's Playing Tonight?" uses. (One paragraph tells the similarities and the other tells the differences.)

4. Direct students to p. 41 and have them complete Activities A and B. Help students as necessary, and invite volunteers to share their answers.

Lesson 4 Balancing Details

1. Say: **In a good compare-and-contrast essay, details that compare or contrast two subjects should be balanced. This means that you should include about the same number of details for each subject or have about the same number of comparisons and contrasts. However, you don't need to have exactly the same number because sometimes things are more alike than different, or more different than alike.**

2. Help students check for balanced details in "What's Playing Tonight?" Have students underline each similarity and double-underline each difference. Then ask: **Is the information balanced?** (yes) **How do you know?** (There are about the same number of similarities as differences.)

Page 41 / Student Book Page 26

Name: _____

Compare-and-Contrast Essay

Organizing Details

A. Organize the details from "What's Playing Tonight?" Write the similarities and differences between movies and plays.

Similarities	Differences
• tell stories • can be entertaining or boring • have a director • have actors	• Plays have been around for thousands of years, but movies have been around for only 100 years. • Plays are performed live, but movies are filmed. • Plays have fewer special effects and settings than movies.

B. Organize the details from "What's Playing Tonight?" by writing details about movies and then details about plays.

Movies	Plays
• entertaining or boring • tell stories • filmed with a camera • have a director • have actors • can be viewed almost anywhere • can have many special effects • can have many settings	• entertaining or boring • tell stories • performed live • have a director • have actors • must be seen where the play is being performed • have fewer actors than movies

© Evan-Moor Corp. • EMC 6015 • Nonfiction Writing EXPOSITORY WRITING **41**

Page 42 / Student Book Page 27

Name: _____

Compare-and-Contrast Essay

Balancing Details

A. The paragraphs below are from a compare-and-contrast essay about two games. Draw a star beside the essay's topic sentence. Underline the details about kickball. Double-underline the details about baseball.

Nothing beats a good game of kickball or baseball. However, there are some ★ things that make these two playground games different. Kickball is played with a large rubber ball. A pitcher rolls the ball on the ground to a player who tries to kick the ball and then run to the bases. Kickball was invented around 1917, but no official rules were ever created for the game.

Some form of baseball has been around since the 1300s. Today in the United States, there are official rules for the game.

B. Is the information above balanced or unbalanced? Explain your answer.

It is unbalanced because there are several more details about kickball than baseball.

C. Complete the chart with details from the paragraphs in Activity A. Then add your own details to balance the information.

Kickball	Baseball
• a playground game • played with a large rubber ball • players kick the ball • pitcher rolls the ball • no official rules • invented around 1917	• a playground game • played with a baseball • players hit the ball with a bat • pitcher throws the ball • has official rules • has been around since 1300s

42 EXPOSITORY WRITING Nonfiction Writing • EMC 6015 • © Evan-Moor Corp.

Writing a Compare-and-Contrast Essay, continued

Page 43 / Student Book Page 28

Name: _____

Compare-and-Contrast Essay

Writing a Conclusion

A. Read each conclusion. Underline the sentence that gives a summary of the subjects. Then write whether the conclusion gives a recommendation, explains why the comparison is important, or states the writer's opinion.

1. <u>Mountain biking and skateboarding are extreme sports that get you moving outside.</u> Whether you want to tear through park trails on a mountain bike or swoosh around a skate park on a skateboard, both sports are fantastic to try.

   This conclusion states the writer's opinion.

2. <u>Both Taste of Persia and Antonio's are excellent restaurants with delicious food.</u> And choosing a restaurant for dinner is a tough decision, so why not try them both?

   This conclusion gives a recommendation.

3. <u>Because of their similarities in color and shape, it is easy to confuse the venomous coral snake with the scarlet king snake.</u> However, knowing the difference between the two can be a matter of life and death for hikers who visit areas where coral snakes live.

   This conclusion explains why the comparison is important.

B. Rewrite the weak conclusion below. Be sure to write a recommendation, explain why the comparison is important, or state your opinion.

   In conclusion, football and soccer are both sports. Many people play them. Some people like one better than the other.

   Many people enjoy playing both football and soccer. But if you just want to be able to run outside with a ball and play a quick game with your friends, then soccer is your best choice.

© Evan-Moor Corp. • EMC 6015 • Nonfiction Writing   EXPOSITORY WRITING   43

Page 44 and Sample Revision / Student Book Page 29

Name: _____

Compare-and-Contrast Essay

Reviewing a Compare-and-Contrast Essay

Revis...
on a...

Focus...

Sample Answer

Two Great Resources

Students who have to research a topic might use the Internet or a magazine. Both are good sources of information, and each has its advantages and disadvantages.

The Internet is easy to use from almost any computer. Students can find articles, pictures, music, and videos to use in their research. They can also connect with other students on the Internet to share or find information. However, a lot of information on the Internet is not always true. People can write almost anything on the Internet. Very few Internet sites check all of their facts.

On the other hand, magazines often have a lot of true information. This is because many people who write and publish the stories and articles in a magazine check their facts. Magazines usually have articles and pictures that students can use in their research. But the right magazines for some topics can be hard to find. Magazines don't have sound or video, either.

When research is necessary, many students turn to the Internet or to magazines. However, students should understand the advantages and disadvantages of both in order to do the best possible research.

---

3. Direct students to Activity A on p. 42 and read the instructions aloud. Model finding one detail about kickball and one detail about baseball. Then have students complete Activities A and B independently. Review the answers as a group.

4. For Activity C, first have students brainstorm traits of baseball and kickball. If necessary, allow students to research facts about the topics. Then have students complete the activity.

Lesson 5 Writing a Conclusion

1. Say: **A compare-and-contrast essay should include a conclusion that sums up the subjects of the essay and how they are similar or different. The conclusion may also state your opinion about the subjects, make a recommendation, or tell why it was important to compare and contrast your subjects.** Ask: **What does the conclusion do in "What's Playing Tonight?"** (It tells why it is important to compare and contrast movies and plays.)

2. Direct students to Activity A on p. 43. Read the instructions aloud and have students complete the activity. Review the answers as a group. Ask students to explain how they knew what the conclusions did.

3. Direct students to Activity B. Read aloud the instructions and the weak conclusion. Help students brainstorm ways to revise the conclusion. Then have students complete the activity. Invite volunteers to share their revised conclusions.

Lesson 6 Reviewing a Compare-and-Contrast Essay

1. Review the qualities of a good compare-and-contrast essay: sentences that compare and contrast, organized details, balanced information, and a conclusion. Have students read "Two Great Resources" on p. 44 and discuss what might be improved. For example, suggest that students draw a chart like the one on p. 42 to organize the details in the essay and to determine if any need to be added. Also, tell students to correct any grammar, punctuation, and spelling errors in the draft.

2. Have students revise the essay independently on a separate sheet of paper. Remind them that there may be different ways to fix the essay. Also remind them to proofread their revisions and check for errors.

3. Invite students to share their revisions with the class.

Name: _____

Introducing a Compare-and-Contrast Essay

Read this example of a compare-and-contrast essay.

What's Playing Tonight?

If you want to see people act out a story, you can go to a movie or a play. Movies and plays have many things in common, but there are some big differences between them, as well.

Movies and plays are both forms of entertainment in which people act out stories. In both cases, actors memorize a script and pretend to be different characters. Movies and plays also have directors who tell the actors where to stand and how to say their lines. In addition, both movies and plays can be funny, sad, exciting, or even a little boring at times.

However, there are many differences between plays and movies. First of all, plays have been around for thousands of years, but movies have been around for only a hundred years or so. Plays are performed live, whereas movies are filmed with cameras and shown to audiences later. Audiences must go to a theater or another special place to see a play. However, people can watch a movie almost anywhere, such as in a theater, in a living room, or even sitting in front of a computer. Another difference is that movies often have more special effects than plays do. And movies can be filmed in many places, which means that the settings can change more often in movies than in plays.

Movies and plays can be equally wonderful, and one isn't better than the other. It just depends on what you feel like seeing. Are you in the mood for the excitement of a live performance, or the special effects and convenience of a movie? Thinking about how movies and plays are alike and different can help you decide what kind of show you want to see.

Writer's Purpose: _____

_____

Name: _____

Writing to Compare and Contrast

A. Read each sentence. Circle the subjects that are being compared or contrasted. Underline the signal word or words that show a comparison or contrast.

1. Both George Washington and John Adams were president of the United States.

2. Gold is a metal. Silver is also a metal, but it is lighter.

3. The moon is cold, while the sun is very hot.

4. Coyotes have several features in common with wolves.

5. Winter in Russia is cold, whereas winter in the Bahamas is warm.

B. Follow the instructions to write a sentence that compares or contrasts each pair of subjects. Use signal words and phrases in your sentences.

> **Example**
>
> Compare decimals and fractions.
>
> _Both decimals and fractions are parts of whole numbers._

1. Compare wasps and bees.

   _____

2. Contrast swimming and running.

   _____

3. Compare the United States and Canada.

   _____

4. Contrast bicycles and skateboards.

   _____

   Nonfiction Writing • EMC 6015 • © Evan-Moor Corp.

Organizing Details

A. Organize the details from "What's Playing Tonight?" Write the similarities and differences between movies and plays.

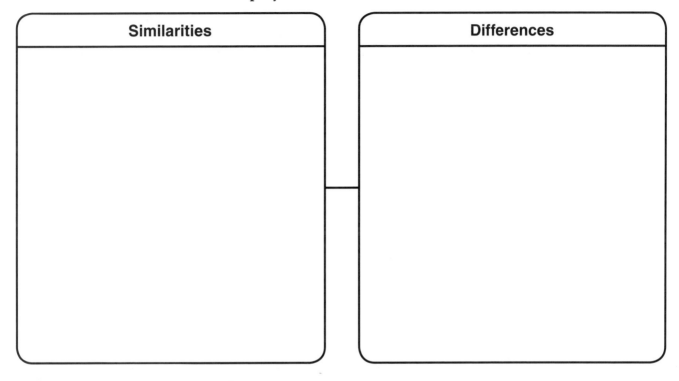

B. Organize the details from "What's Playing Tonight?" by writing details about movies and then details about plays.

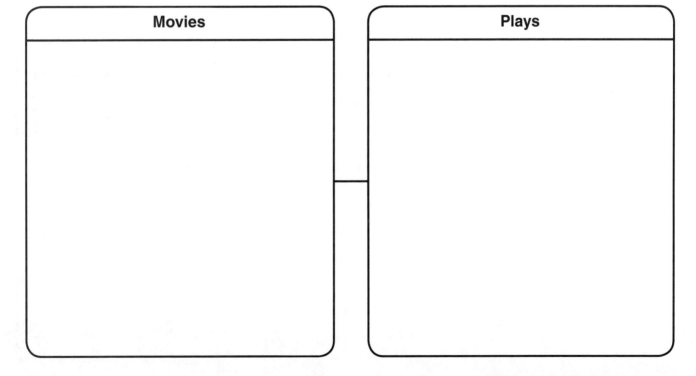

Name: _____

Balancing Details

A. The paragraphs below are from a compare-and-contrast essay about two games. Draw a star beside the essay's topic sentence. Underline the details about kickball. Double-underline the details about baseball.

> Nothing beats a good game of kickball or baseball. However, there are some things that make these two playground games different. Kickball is played with a large rubber ball. A pitcher rolls the ball on the ground to a player who tries to kick the ball and then run to the bases. Kickball was invented around 1917, but no official rules were ever created for the game.
>
> Some form of baseball has been around since the 1300s. Today in the United States, there are official rules for the game.

B. Is the information above balanced or unbalanced? Explain your answer.

_____

_____

C. Complete the chart with details from the paragraphs in Activity A. Then add your own details to balance the information.

Kickball	Baseball

Writing a Conclusion

A. Read each conclusion. Underline the sentence that gives a summary of the subjects. Then write whether the conclusion gives a recommendation, explains why the comparison is important, or states the writer's opinion.

1.   Mountain biking and skateboarding are extreme sports that get you moving outside. Whether you want to tear through park trails on a mountain bike or swoosh around a skate park on a skateboard, both sports are fantastic to try.

_____

2.   Both Taste of Persia and Antonio's are excellent restaurants with delicious food. And choosing a restaurant for dinner is a tough decision, so why not try them both?

_____

3.   Because of their similarities in color and shape, it is easy to confuse the venomous coral snake with the scarlet king snake. However, knowing the difference between the two can be a matter of life and death for hikers who visit areas where coral snakes live.

_____

B. Rewrite the weak conclusion below. Be sure to write a recommendation, explain why the comparison is important, or state your opinion.

   In conclusion, football and soccer are both sports. Many people play them. Some people like one better than the other.

_____

_____

_____

_____

_____

Reviewing a Compare-and-Contrast Essay

Revise this essay. Use what you have learned to make it stronger. Rewrite the essay on a separate sheet of paper.

Focus on:

✓ writing sentences that compare and contrast
✓ organizing the details into paragraphs
✓ balancing the number of details
✓ writing a conclusion that summarizes the subjects and states an opinion, gives a recommendation, or explains why the comparison is important
✓ correcting grammar, spelling, and punctuation errors

Draft

Two Great Resources

Students who have to research a topic might use the Internet or a magazine. Both are good sources of information. Each has its advantages and disadvantages.

The Internet is easy to use. From almost any computer. Students can find articles, pictures, music, and videos to use in their research. Maps and photos are easily found. Magazines usually have articles and pictures that students can use in their research. Students can also conect with each other on the Internet to share information. However, a lot of information. On the Internet is not accurate or true. People cans writes or says anything on the Internet. Not every fact is checked.

Magazines also have a lot of factual information. It is usually correct. People who write and publish the stories and articles in magazines check their facts. But there's no video.

In conclusion, the Internet and magazines are both good.

Writing a Biography

Lesson 1 Introducing a Biography

A biography is a true story about a real person in which important information and major events from that person's life are described in sequential order.

1. Remind students that a biography is writing that describes true and important events from someone's life. Then have students read the model on p. 48.

2. Have students identify the subject of the biography. (Jane Goodall) Then ask: **What is the purpose of this biography?** (to tell about the life of Jane Goodall) Have students write the purpose on the lines provided.

3. Invite students to offer opinions about what makes this a good biography. Prompt students by asking: **Does the writer clearly state who this biography is about and why she is important? Do the main ideas from each paragraph tell you something important about Jane Goodall's life? Are the events organized in the order in which they occurred?** Then explain that students will use the model as they practice the skills needed to write a good biography.

➤ **Extend the Lesson:** Have students brainstorm types of people, such as scientists, athletes, actors, writers, or explorers who would make interesting subjects. Then encourage students to think of specific people in each category who interest them most.

Lesson 2 Organizing Details

1. Say: **When you write a biography, details about your subject should be written in chronological order, or the order in which they occurred. Often, a biography begins with the person's birth and ends with his or her death. If the person is still alive, the biography describes what he or she is doing currently.**

2. Have students reread the writing model on p. 48. Then ask: **Are the details in chronological order?** (yes)

3. Direct students to p. 49. Have them complete Activities A and B independently or in pairs. For Activity B, remind students that their sentences should flow and sound like a cohesive paragraph, so they should not simply be copied from Activity A. Invite students to share their paragraphs.

➤ **Extend the Lesson:** Have students find and list details to include in a biography about the person they selected in the Lesson 1 extension activity. Have them write or number the details in chronological order.

© Evan-Moor Corp. • EMC 6015 • Nonfiction Writing

EXPOSITORY WRITING 45

Page 48 / Student Book Page 31

Name: _____

Biography

Introducing a Biography
Read this example of a biography.

> **Writing Model**
>
> #### Chimp Champ
>
> Jane Goodall changed the way the world thinks about chimpanzees. She discovered important things about these African animals by watching them in their natural habitats.
>
> Jane Goodall was born in 1934. Even as a child, she dreamed of visiting Africa. Jane's favorite toy was a stuffed chimpanzee named Jubilee. And her favorite book was *Tarzan*, which is set in Africa. So when a friend invited Jane to visit her in Africa in 1957, Jane knew she had to go.
>
> The trip to Africa changed Jane's life forever. There, she met Dr. Louis Leakey, a famous scientist. She became Dr. Leakey's assistant. In 1960, Dr. Leakey asked Jane to study a group of wild chimpanzees that lived in Gombe National Park.
>
> Jane accepted the job gladly. Jane made several important discoveries about chimps. She first discovered that chimps used sticks as tools. She saw them use the sticks to get termites out of their nests. Until this time, scientists believed that only people used tools. Jane's second discovery was that chimpanzees hunted other mammals for food. Everyone had thought that chimps ate only plants and insects. Jane spent the next 25 years studying chimps in Africa, and she became the world's expert.
>
> In 1977, Jane founded the Jane Goodall Institute. She wanted to protect great apes and their habitats. For over 30 years, Jane has talked to people everywhere about chimps. And she has met with hundreds of government officials about conserving chimp habitats.
>
> Jane still goes back to Gombe to visit her chimpanzee friends. She is a tireless woman who will never stop protecting the animals she has loved since childhood. And she still has Jubilee, the stuffed toy that started it all!

Writer's Purpose: to tell about the life of Jane Goodall

_____

48 EXPOSITORY WRITING   Nonfiction Writing • EMC 6015 • © Evan-Moor Corp.

Page 49 / Student Book Page 32

Name: _____

Biography

Organizing Details

A. Read the sentences below about Ada Byron. Number the events in chronological order.

  2 Ada studied math, music, and science when she was young.

  6 Ada died of cancer in 1852. Although Babbage's machine was never built, it is often considered to be the world's first computer. Ada's notes live on as the first computer program.

  5 In 1842 and 1843, Ada translated a book about Babbage's machine. She included math problems that she wanted the machine to solve.

  1 Ada Byron was born in England on December 10, 1815.

  4 Ada and Babbage became good friends, and she began working for Babbage.

  3 Ada met the mathematician Charles Babbage in 1833. He designed a new kind of math machine that could solve math problems.

B. Write a paragraph that tells about Ada Byron's life in chronological order.

Ada Byron was born in England on December 10, 1815. She studied math, music, and science as she grew up. In 1833, she met the mathematician Charles Babbage. He had designed a new kind of math machine that could solve math problems. Ada and Babbage became good friends. In 1842 and 1843, Ada translated a book about the machine and added notes that had math problems she wanted the machine to solve. Ada Byron died of cancer in 1852. Babbage's machine was never built, but it is often called the world's first computer. Ada's notes live on as the world's first computer program.

© Evan-Moor Corp. • EMC 6015 • Nonfiction Writing   EXPOSITORY WRITING 49

Writing a Biography, continued

Page 50 / Student Book Page 33

Name: _____

Biography

Writing Main-Idea Sentences

Read each paragraph. Then use the details from the paragraph to revise the underlined main-idea sentence. Make sure each main-idea sentence matches the details in the paragraph.

Example

> <u>Mark Twain lived in many places.</u> When he was 11, he became an apprentice for a newspaper in Missouri. Seven years later, he wrote for newspapers in New York and Philadelphia.
>
> *Mark Twain worked for several newspapers.*

1. <u>Mark Twain liked boats.</u> As a young man, Twain worked on a steamboat. It traveled up and down the Mississippi River. After that, he went to Nevada with his brother to look for silver. Twain moved to San Francisco, California, in 1864. And when he became a famous writer, Twain toured many cities in the United States and Europe.

   Mark Twain traveled throughout his life.

2. <u>Twain was a famous writer.</u> His stories are set in locations from Connecticut to California. He is most famous for *The Adventures of Tom Sawyer* and *The Adventures of Huckleberry Finn*. These novels are about two boys who lived in the South. Twain is also famous for writing his views about people and politics in the United States.

   Twain wrote about American life.

3. <u>Mark Twain knew several scientists.</u> In the 1890s, he was good friends with the famous engineer Nikola Tesla. Thomas Edison visited Twain in 1909. And Twain himself invented three products, including a scrapbook with glue already on the pages.

   Mark Twain was interested in science and inventing things.

4. <u>Mark Twain was a writer and a speaker.</u> He earned money from his popular books and spent a lot of it on a printing machine. The machine was great when it worked, but it broke down a lot, which cost him money. He also lost money by publishing books himself. His first book was a success, but others were not. One of the books he published sold fewer than two hundred copies.

   Mark Twain had some money troubles.

50 EXPOSITORY WRITING

Nonfiction Writing • EMC 6015 • © Evan-Moor Corp.

Lesson 3 Writing Main-Idea Sentences

1. Activate prior knowledge by asking volunteers to explain what the main idea in a paragraph is. (what the paragraph is mostly about) Say: **In a biography, each body paragraph usually tells readers about a different part of a person's life. These paragraphs often have a sentence that tells the main idea.**

2. Have students work in small groups to find and underline the sentences that tell the main idea in paragraphs 2 through 5 of the model on p. 48. (the second sentence in paragraphs 2 and 5; the third sentence in paragraph 3; the first sentence in paragraph 4) Say: **The main idea in paragraph 2 is Jane's love of Africa as a child. The main idea in paragraph 3 is about becoming Dr. Leakey's assistant. The main idea in paragraph 4 is about Jane's work protecting chimps. The details in each of these paragraphs support the sentences that tell these main ideas.**

3. Direct students to p. 50. If necessary, explain that Mark Twain was a famous American writer. Read aloud the example. Point out that the topic sentence does not focus on the main idea of the paragraph, that Twain worked for newspapers. The revision is better because it states the main idea of the entire paragraph.

4. Have students complete the activity independently or in pairs. Suggest that they first find the main idea of each paragraph to help them decide how to revise the underlined sentences. Remind them that there is more than one way to revise each sentence. Invite students to share their revised sentences.

➤ **Extend the Lesson:** Remind students of the details they organized in the Lesson 2 extension activity. Then have them write a sentence for the details that are related. (e.g., details about someone's childhood)

Lesson 4 Removing Unnecessary Details

1. Review the purpose of a biography. Then say: **As you research, you will read a lot of details about your subject. However, you do not need to include them all in your biography. Too many details and too much information can be confusing.**

2. Have students review the writing model on p. 48. Say: **One detail not mentioned is that Jane Goodall named all of the chimpanzees she observed. Why do you think the author left out this detail?** (This is a short biography about Goodall's life, so the names of the chimps are unnecessary.)

3. Remind students that a biography focuses on the life of one person. Therefore, it should not include too many details about other people. Say: **This biography of Jane Goodall mentions Louis Leakey because he was important in her life. However, the author did not include many details about Leakey's life because they are not about Jane Goodall.**

4. Have students complete Activity A on p. 51 in pairs. Invite volunteers to read each revised paragraph aloud. Then discuss why each crossed-out detail was unnecessary.

5. Have students complete Activity B independently or in pairs. Remind students to make sure their paragraph has a topic sentence and that their sentences flow. Invite volunteers to read their paragraphs aloud. Discuss which details were left out and why.

➤ **Extend the Lesson:** In pairs, have students interview and write a short biography of each other. Ask students to include one or two pieces of unnecessary information. Then have each pair trade biographies with another pair and cross out the unnecessary details in those biographies.

Lesson 5 Reviewing a Biography

1. Review the qualities of a good biography: interesting and important information about a real person, chronological order of events, paragraphs that tell about a part of a person's life that are organized with good details and a sentence that tells the main idea, and no unnecessary details. Have students read "A Towering Life" on p. 52 and discuss what might be improved. For example, suggest that they read through the biography first, cross out unnecessary details, and then number the remaining details in chronological order. Also, tell students to correct any grammar, punctuation, and spelling errors in the draft.

2. Have students revise the biography independently on a separate sheet of paper. Remind them that there are different ways to fix the biography. Also remind them to proofread their revisions and check for errors.

3. Invite students to share their revisions with the class.

Page 51 / Student Book Page 34

Name: _____   Biography

Removing Unnecessary Details

A. Read the paragraphs below from a biography of Louis Armstrong. Cross out any unnecessary details.

Louis Armstrong is one of the most famous jazz musicians of all time. He played the trumpet and sang. He is known for his scratchy, deep voice, which many people today still love. ~~Many people like jazz better than other kinds of music.~~

Armstrong grew up in New Orleans, Louisiana. ~~Baton Rouge is the capital of Louisiana.~~ As a child, he sang on the streets for money. When he was 12, he met his first music teacher, Peter Davis. Davis taught Armstrong how to play the cornet (a type of trumpet) and other instruments. ~~Armstrong never played the violin.~~

When he grew up, Armstrong played with different bands in Chicago. ~~The Great Chicago Fire took place in 1871.~~ Then he joined King Oliver's Creole Jazz Band. Armstrong's cornet solos quickly became famous. He played in New York and then toured through Europe. ~~Europe is a continent.~~ Soon, he was playing across the world.

B. Use the notes below to write a paragraph about the famous singer and actress Lena Horne. Leave out any unnecessary details.

- She was born in 1917 in New York City.
- She began singing and dancing at age 16.
- She moved to Hollywood in 1941 and was in movies, including *Stormy Weather* and *The Wiz*.
- Her granddaughter is a screenwriter.
- By the 1950s, she focused on her singing career.
- She won many awards.
- Sidney Lumet directed *The Wiz*.
- Horne died in 2010.

Lena Horne was a famous singer and actress who won many awards. She was born in 1917 in New York City. She began singing and dancing when she was 16. She moved to Hollywood in 1941 and appeared in movies, including *Stormy Weather* and *The Wiz*. By the 1950s, she decided to focus on her singing career. Lena Horne died in 2010.

© Evan-Moor Corp. • EMC 6015 • Nonfiction Writing   **EXPOSITORY WRITING** 51

Page 52 and Sample Revision / Student Book Page 35

Name: _____   Biography

Reviewing a Biography

Sample Answer

A Towering Life

Gustave Eiffel was a famous French engineer. He built many buildings and bridges. His most famous building is the Eiffel Tower, the symbol of Paris.

Eiffel was born in 1832. His family was rich, so Eiffel was able to go to good schools in France. He studied science, history, literature, and chemistry.

Eiffel had a successful career. In 1855, he joined a company that made bridges. He helped build many bridges, and he learned how to run a business. He formed his own company in 1867. He designed and built buildings and bridges around the world. In 1885, he designed the inside of the Statue of Liberty. And from 1887 to 1889, he built the Eiffel Tower.

Gustave Eiffel died in 1923. He had built more than 60 bridges and buildings in his lifetime. But his most famous building is the one that shares his name—the Eiffel Tower.

Introducing a Biography

Read this example of a biography.

Writing Model

Chimp Champ

Jane Goodall changed the way the world thinks about chimpanzees. She discovered important things about these African animals by watching them in their natural habitats.

Jane Goodall was born in 1934. Even as a child, she dreamed of visiting Africa. Jane's favorite toy was a stuffed chimpanzee named Jubilee. And her favorite book was *Tarzan*, which is set in Africa. So when a friend invited Jane to visit her in Africa in 1957, Jane knew she had to go.

The trip to Africa changed Jane's life forever. There, she met Dr. Louis Leakey, a famous scientist. She became Dr. Leakey's assistant. In 1960, Dr. Leakey asked Jane to study a group of wild chimpanzees that lived in Gombe National Park.

Jane accepted the job gladly. Jane made several important discoveries about chimps. She first discovered that chimps used sticks as tools. She saw them use the sticks to get termites out of their nests. Until this time, scientists believed that only people used tools. Jane's second discovery was that chimpanzees hunted other mammals for food. Everyone had thought that chimps ate only plants and insects. Jane spent the next 25 years studying chimps in Africa, and she became the world's expert.

In 1977, Jane founded the Jane Goodall Institute. She wanted to protect great apes and their habitats. For over 30 years, Jane has talked to people everywhere about chimps. And she has met with hundreds of government officials about conserving chimp habitats.

Jane still goes back to Gombe to visit her chimpanzee friends. She is a tireless woman who will never stop protecting the animals she has loved since childhood. And she still has Jubilee, the stuffed toy that started it all!

Writer's Purpose: _____

_____

Organizing Details

A. Read the sentences below about Ada Byron. Number the events in chronological order.

_____ Ada studied math, music, and science when she was young.

_____ Ada died of cancer in 1852. Although Babbage's machine was never built, it is often considered to be the world's first computer. Ada's notes live on as the first computer program.

_____ In 1842 and 1843, Ada translated a book about Babbage's machine. She included math problems that she wanted the machine to solve.

_____ Ada Byron was born in England on December 10, 1815.

_____ Ada and Babbage became good friends, and she began working for Babbage.

_____ Ada met the mathematician Charles Babbage in 1833. He designed a new kind of math machine that could solve math problems.

B. Write a paragraph that tells about Ada Byron's life in chronological order.

_____

_____

_____

_____

_____

_____

_____

_____

_____

_____

_____

Name: _____

Writing Main-Idea Sentences

Read each paragraph. Then use the details from the paragraph to revise the underlined main-idea sentence. Make sure each main-idea sentence matches the details in the paragraph.

Example

Mark Twain lived in many places. When he was 11, he became an apprentice for a newspaper in Missouri. Seven years later, he wrote for newspapers in New York and Philadelphia.

Mark Twain worked for several newspapers.

1. Mark Twain liked boats. As a young man, Twain worked on a steamboat. It traveled up and down the Mississippi River. After that, he went to Nevada with his brother to look for silver. Twain moved to San Francisco, California, in 1864. And when he became a famous writer, Twain toured many cities in the United States and Europe.

_____

2. Twain was a famous writer. His stories are set in locations from Connecticut to California. He is most famous for *The Adventures of Tom Sawyer* and *The Adventures of Huckleberry Finn.* These novels are about two boys who lived in the South. Twain is also famous for writing his views about people and politics in the United States.

_____

3. Mark Twain knew several scientists. In the 1890s, he was good friends with the famous engineer Nikola Tesla. Thomas Edison visited Twain in 1909. And Twain himself invented three products, including a scrapbook with glue already on the pages.

_____

4. Mark Twain was a writer and a speaker. He earned money from his popular books and spent a lot of it on a printing machine. The machine was great when it worked, but it broke down a lot, which cost him money. He also lost money by publishing books himself. His first book was a success, but others were not. One of the books he published sold fewer than two hundred copies.

_____

Removing Unnecessary Details

A. Read the paragraphs below from a biography of Louis Armstrong.
   Cross out any unnecessary details.

   Louis Armstrong is one of the most famous jazz musicians of all time. He played the trumpet and sang. He is known for his scratchy, deep voice, which many people today still love. Many people like jazz better than other kinds of music.

   Armstrong grew up in New Orleans, Louisiana. Baton Rouge is the capital of Louisiana. As a child, he sang on the streets for money. When he was 12, he met his first music teacher, Peter Davis. Davis taught Armstrong how to play the cornet (a type of trumpet) and other instruments. Armstrong never played the violin.

   When he grew up, Armstrong played with different bands in Chicago. The Great Chicago Fire took place in 1871. Then he joined King Oliver's Creole Jazz Band. Armstrong's cornet solos quickly became famous. He played in New York and then toured through Europe. Europe is a continent. Soon, he was playing across the world.

B. Use the notes below to write a paragraph about the famous singer and actress Lena Horne. Leave out any unnecessary details.

   - She was born in 1917 in New York City.
   - She began singing and dancing at age 16.
   - She moved to Hollywood in 1941 and was in movies, including *Stormy Weather* and *The Wiz*.
   - Her granddaughter is a screenwriter.

   - By the 1950s, she focused on her singing career.
   - She won many awards.
   - Sidney Lumet directed *The Wiz*.
   - Horne died in 2010.

   _____

   _____

   _____

   _____

   _____

   _____

   _____

Name: _____

Reviewing a Biography

Revise this biography. Use what you have learned to make it stronger.
Rewrite the biography on a separate sheet of paper.

Focus on:

✓ writing a sentence that tells the main idea of each paragraph
✓ organizing details in chronological order
✓ removing unnecessary details
✓ correcting grammar, punctuation, and spelling errors

Draft

A Towering Life

Gustave Eiffel was a famoos French engineer. French is spoken in France and parts of Canada. He is most famoos for the Eiffel Tower. It is now a symbol of Paris. Paris are a popular city to visit.

Eiffel had a successful career. Then, in 1867 he formed his own company. In 1855, Eiffel, started working for a company. The company made bridges. He helped build many bridges. And learned how to run a business. Eiffel almost worked for a vinegar company.

Eiffel and his new company designed and built buildings and bridges around the world. Eiffel did not build the longest bridge in the world, which is in Japan. From 1887 to 1889, he builded the Eiffel Tower. And in 1885, he dezigned the inside of the Statchoo of Liberty.

His family was rich, so Eiffel was able to go to good schools in France when he was young. He studied science, history, literature, and chemistry. Science today is very different compared to science in Eiffel's time.

Gustave Eiffel died in 1923. Gustave Eiffel was born in 1832.

He had built more than 60 bridges and buildings. In his lifetime. But his most famoos building are the one that shares his name—the Eiffel Tower.

Writing a News Article

Lesson 1 Introducing a News Article

A news article is a report that gives factual information about a current event. It should answer the 5Ws and H (who, what, where, when, why, and how) about the event.

1. Explain that a news article gives readers accurate facts and details about a current event. Say: **News articles are useful for telling people about something that has just happened.** Invite students to name recent news events they have heard or read about.

2. Have a volunteer read aloud the model on p. 56. Then ask: **What is the purpose of this news article?** (to tell about Koji Nagano catching a runaway dog) Have students write the purpose on the lines provided.

3. Invite students to offer opinions about what makes this a good news article. Prompt students by asking: **Does the first sentence tell readers what the article is about? Does the writer give all of the basic details about the event? Do you learn the writer's opinions about the event?** Then explain that students will use the model as they practice the skills needed to write a good news article.

➤ **Extend the Lesson:** Have students read news articles from a local or national newspaper. Then have them identify the topic and purpose of each article.

Page 56 / Student Book Page 37

Name: _____

News Article

Introducing a News Article

Read this example of a news article.

> **Writing Model**
>
> **Student Saves Runaway Dog**
>
> Yesterday, local fifth grader Koji Nagano saved a runaway dog at Halibut State Beach.
>
> Leona Miller was walking down a trail to the beach with her terrier, Dobie, around 1:00 P.M. When they reached the beach, Dobie suddenly lunged after a sea gull, pulling his leash out of Ms. Miller's hand. Ms. Miller called out to Dobie, but the dog just kept running toward the busy parking lot.
>
> Koji Nagano had come to the beach with his parents. He was getting a sandwich from the family car when he noticed a gray dog speeding toward him. Then he saw Ms. Miller chasing the dog. Koji opened the car door, called to the dog, and threw his sandwich into the back seat. Dobie leapt into the car, and Koji quickly shut the door to keep Dobie from escaping. Ms. Miller then retrieved Dobie from the car.
>
> Lifeguard Alison Early said she has seen several dogs run away from their owners at the beach. "Dog owners should take extra care when bringing their pets here," she said.
>
> Ms. Miller said she was grateful to Koji for saving her beloved Dobie. "Koji was kind and quick-thinking," Ms. Miller said. "I should buy him a new sandwich."

Writer's Purpose: to tell about Koji Nagano catching a runaway dog

Lesson 2 Answering the 5Ws and H

1. Review the purpose of a news article. Then say: **A news reporter gives readers all of the information about an event by answering a few basic questions: Who? What? Where? When? Why? How? We call these questions the "5Ws and H."** Emphasize that each question can have more than one answer, and that sometimes a reporter is only able to answer some of the questions.

2. Guide students through the writing model on p. 56 to identify the 5Ws and H. Emphasize the first word of each question as you ask: **What happened?** (A boy caught a runaway dog.) **Who caught the dog?** (Koji Nagano) **Who lost the dog?** (Leona Miller) **Where did the boy catch the dog?** (in the parking lot of Halibut State Beach) **When did it happen?** (yesterday at 1:00 P.M.) **Why did the dog run away?** (It was chasing a sea gull.) **How did Koji stop the dog?** (He threw a sandwich into the car to get the dog to jump in after it.)

Page 57 / Student Book Page 38

Name: _____

News Article

Answering the 5Ws and H

Complete the chart with details about an event that recently took place at your school. Use the 5Ws and H to think of good questions to answer about the event.

Event: <u>teacher showed students photos of Mayan ruins</u>

Who <u>was involved in the photo show</u> ?	Mr. York, fifth-grade students
What <u>happened during the photo show</u> ?	Mr. York showed students 50 photos from his trip to Mayan ruins in South America.
Where <u>did the photo show take place</u> ?	in Mr. York's classroom at Spellman Elementary
When <u>did the photo show happen</u> ?	last Monday, May 9
Why <u>did the teacher show the photos</u> ?	The class is studying the ancient Maya.
How <u>did the teacher present the photos</u> ?	He displayed photos on a large screen and told students about them.

© Evan-Moor Corp. • EMC 6015 • Nonfiction Writing **EXPOSITORY WRITING 57**

Page 58 / Student Book Page 39

Name: _____

News Article

Writing a Good Lead

A. Read each pair of sentences. Underline the sentence that is a better lead for a news article.

1. A helicopter is an aircraft that uses spinning blades called rotors to lift into the air.
   <u>Yesterday morning, a helicopter safely made an emergency landing in a school field.</u>

2. <u>After a very close election, Monica Gomez was elected school president last week.</u>
   Monica Gomez probably won the election because she promised better school lunches.

3. A big fire burned brightly last night somewhere on an old farm.
   <u>A fire started last night when lightning struck an old barn in Miller County.</u>

B. Read each paragraph. Revise the underlined lead to make it include as many answers to the 5Ws and H as possible.

1. <u>Last night, somebody found some keys.</u> After closing his auto shop for the day, Adam Cherniak walked home. On the way, he noticed something shiny on the sidewalk. When he realized it was a set of keys, he took them to the police. Jonas Mars had reported the keys missing two days earlier.

   <u>Last night, a local mechanic found a set of missing car keys.</u>

2. <u>The storm was bad.</u> The strong rainstorm began late yesterday afternoon and continued for several hours. More than two inches of rain fell during the storm. Several streets in Yuma were flooded, causing long traffic delays. Businesses on Main Street in Yuma were closed all day. No injuries have been reported.

   <u>A storm caused floods and other problems in Yuma last night.</u>

3. <u>At noon yesterday, there was a nice ceremony.</u> Principal Naomi Miller gave a short speech. She thanked the designers, workers, and parents. Then she cut the ribbon and the happy crowd applauded the new Howard School playground. Students scrambled all over the climbing bars while parents toured the new field.

   <u>A new playground at Howard School opened yesterday at noon with a ribbon-cutting ceremony.</u>

3. Direct students to the chart on p. 57. Help students brainstorm a current event at school that they can write about for the activity (e.g., a field trip).

4. If necessary, help students phrase the 5W-and-H questions for the chart. Then have students answer the questions with details about the event. Invite volunteers to share what they wrote.

➤ **Extend the Lesson:** Have students use their completed charts to write one or more sentences about the event.

Lesson 3 Writing a Good Lead

1. Say: **The first sentence in a news article is called the *lead*. It should grab the reader's attention and answer as many of the 5Ws and H as possible.**

2. Have a volunteer identify the lead in the model on p. 56 and point out the 5Ws and H that are answered by it. (when, who, what, where)

3. Direct students to Activity A on p. 58. Ask a volunteer to read aloud the two sentences for item 1. Ask: **Which sentence is a stronger lead?** (the second) **Why?** (It tells what happened, where the helicopter landed, and when it happened. The first sentence just states a fact.) Have students complete the activity in pairs. Discuss the answers.

4. Read aloud the directions for Activity B. Have students complete the activity independently or in pairs. Ask volunteers to share their leads with the class and explain why they are better than the originals.

➤ **Extend the Lesson:** Provide students with copies of news articles from a local newspaper that have the leads blacked out. Have students write leads for those articles.

Lesson 4 Using a Neutral Voice

1. Review the purpose of a news article. Then say: **A news article tells the main details of an event, but it does not tell the writer's opinions or feelings about the event. A good news article should have a neutral, or unbiased, voice.**

2. Have students review the writing model on p. 56 and discuss the voice of the article. Point out that the reporter does not give any strong personal opinions, and she does not show a bias for or against the event in the article.

3. Read the directions and the first sentence of the article in Activity A on p. 59. Ask: **Which words show opinion or bias?** *(wonderful, beautiful)* **Cross out those words.** Have students complete the activity in pairs or independently. Then invite volunteers to read the edited article aloud and to explain why they crossed out some words or sentences.

4. Have students complete Activity B independently or in pairs. Invite volunteers to share their revisions. Ask the class if each revision uses a neutral voice.

➤ **Extend the Lesson:** Have students look through a newspaper to compare news articles with editorial or opinion pieces, preferably on the same topic. Challenge students to find words or phrases from the editorial or opinion piece that show bias.

Lesson 5   Reviewing a News Article

1. Review the qualities of a good news article: details that answer the 5Ws and H, a strong lead, and a neutral voice.

2. Have students read "Declaration of Independence Adopted" on p. 60. Explain that the article is written as if the event had just happened. Then discuss how the article might be improved. For example, ask students if the article answers all of the 5Ws and H. (It does not. It does not tell specifically what was signed or when it was signed.) Also, tell students to correct any grammar, punctuation, and spelling errors in the draft.

3. Have students revise the news article independently on a separate sheet of paper. Remind them that there are different ways to fix the news article. Also remind them to proofread their revisions and check for errors.

4. Invite students to share their revisions with the class.

Page 59 / Student Book Page 40

Name: _____   News Article

Using a Neutral Voice

A. Cross out any words or sentences that do not belong in a news article because they show the writer's bias or personal opinions.

Local Student Finds Bones in Backyard

Local fifth grader Silvana Ayles made a ~~wonderful~~ discovery while digging in her ~~beautiful~~ yard last week. She was ~~doing a great job~~ digging a two-foot hole for a new vegetable garden when her shovel hit something ~~really weird~~. She began to dig more carefully and soon uncovered a bone. ~~I would have stopped right away because bones are creepy. But Silvana was really brave.~~ She kept digging. Soon, she had uncovered six large bones. She showed the bones to her neighbor, Len Owens. He is a researcher at the Natural History Museum. ~~Mr. Owens is the smartest man in town.~~ He says the bones are probably from a horse.

B. Rewrite each statement, using a reporter's neutral voice.

> **Example**
> Two unlucky bicyclists were injured in a horrible accident yesterday.
> Two bicyclists were injured in a serious accident yesterday.

1. I saw the most enormous hawk flying above spooky Miller Creek last weekend.
   A large hawk was seen flying above Miller Creek last weekend.

2. The remarkable Mark Johnson was reelected mayor for the third time because smart voters liked him more than the other rotten candidates.
   Mark Johnson was reelected mayor for the third time. He received more votes than the other candidates.

3. Lunch was finally served at 2:30 after a ridiculously long wait due to a kitchen fire.
   Due to a kitchen fire, lunch was delayed until 2:30.

Page 60 and Sample Revision / Student Book Page 41

Name: _____   News Article

Sample Answer

Declaration of Independence Adopted

On July 4, representatives from America's thirteen colonies met in Philadelphia to adopt the Declaration of Independence. The Declaration states that the United States of America is its own country and is no longer controlled by Great Britain or King George.

A committee of five men wrote the statement declaring independence. Those men asked Thomas Jefferson to write the first draft. He wrote the essay over two weeks in June. It was then revised and edited by Benjamin Franklin and John Adams.

The Declaration tells why the United States should be its own country and not part of Great Britain. It states that the people of the new United States are angry with King George. It then lists all of his deeds that the people disagree with. The Declaration also names the rights that the representatives think all people should have.

The signers of the Declaration of Independence said they believe in the United States of America, and that its people deserve "life, liberty, and the pursuit of happiness."

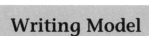

Introducing a News Article

Read this example of a news article.

Writing Model

Student Saves Runaway Dog

Yesterday, local fifth grader Koji Nagano saved a runaway dog at Halibut State Beach.

Leona Miller was walking down a trail to the beach with her terrier, Dobie, around 1:00 P.M. When they reached the beach, Dobie suddenly lunged after a sea gull, pulling his leash out of Ms. Miller's hand. Ms. Miller called out to Dobie, but the dog just kept running toward the busy parking lot.

Koji Nagano had come to the beach with his parents. He was getting a sandwich from the family car when he noticed a gray dog speeding toward him. Then he saw Ms. Miller chasing the dog. Koji opened the car door, called to the dog, and threw his sandwich into the back seat. Dobie leapt into the car, and Koji quickly shut the door to keep Dobie from escaping. Ms. Miller then retrieved Dobie from the car.

Lifeguard Alison Early said she has seen several dogs run away from their owners at the beach. "Dog owners should take extra care when bringing their pets here," she said.

Ms. Miller said she was grateful to Koji for saving her beloved Dobie. "Koji was kind and quick-thinking," Ms. Miller said. "I should buy him a new sandwich."

Writer's Purpose: _____

_____

Answering the 5Ws and H

Complete the chart with details about an event that recently took place at your school. Use the 5Ws and H to think of good questions to answer about the event.

Event: _____	
Who _____ _____?	
What _____ _____?	
Where _____ _____?	
When _____ _____?	
Why _____ _____?	
How _____ _____?	

Writing a Good Lead

A. Read each pair of sentences. Underline the sentence that is a better lead for a news article.

1. A helicopter is an aircraft that uses spinning blades called rotors to lift into the air.
   Yesterday morning, a helicopter safely made an emergency landing in a school field.

2. After a very close election, Monica Gomez was elected school president last week.
   Monica Gomez probably won the election because she promised better school lunches.

3. A big fire burned brightly last night somewhere on an old farm.
   A fire started last night when lightning struck an old barn in Miller County.

B. Read each paragraph. Revise the underlined lead to make it include as many answers to the 5Ws and H as possible.

1. Last night, somebody found some keys. After closing his auto shop for the day, Adam Cherniak walked home. On the way, he noticed something shiny on the sidewalk. When he realized it was a set of keys, he took them to the police. Jonas Mars had reported the keys missing two days earlier.

   _____

2. The storm was bad. The strong rainstorm began late yesterday afternoon and continued for several hours. More than two inches of rain fell during the storm. Several streets in Yuma were flooded, causing long traffic delays. Businesses on Main Street in Yuma were closed all day. No injuries have been reported.

   _____

3. At noon yesterday, there was a nice ceremony. Principal Naomi Miller gave a short speech. She thanked the designers, workers, and parents. Then she cut the ribbon and the happy crowd applauded the new Howard School playground. Students scrambled all over the climbing bars while parents toured the new field.

   _____

   _____

Using a Neutral Voice

A. Cross out any words or sentences that do not belong in a news article because they show the writer's bias or personal opinions.

Local Student Finds Bones in Backyard

Local fifth grader Silvana Ayles made a wonderful discovery while digging in her beautiful yard last week. She was doing a great job digging a two-foot hole for a new vegetable garden when her shovel hit something really weird. She began to dig more carefully and soon uncovered a bone. I would have stopped right away because bones are creepy. But Silvana was really brave. She kept digging. Soon, she had uncovered six large bones. She showed the bones to her neighbor, Len Owens. He is a researcher at the Natural History Museum. Mr. Owens is the smartest man in town. He says the bones are probably from a horse.

B. Rewrite each statement, using a reporter's neutral voice.

> **Example**
>
> Two unlucky bicyclists were injured in a horrible accident yesterday.
>
> <u>Two bicyclists were injured in a serious accident yesterday.</u>

1. I saw the most enormous hawk flying above spooky Miller Creek last weekend.

    _____

    _____

2. The remarkable Mark Johnson was reelected mayor for the third time because smart voters liked him more than the other rotten candidates.

    _____

    _____

3. Lunch was finally served at 2:30 after a ridiculously long wait due to a kitchen fire.

    _____

    _____

Reviewing a News Article

Revise this imaginary news article from 1776. Use what you have learned to make it stronger. Rewrite the article on a separate sheet of paper.

Focus on:
- ✓ writing a good lead
- ✓ answering the 5Ws and H
- ✓ using a neutral voice
- ✓ correcting grammar, spelling, and punctuation errors

Draft

Declaration of Independence Adopted

I just saw something big happen! Representatives from America's 13 colonies met in Philadelphia to sign an exciting document. The document declares that the United States of America is it's own country, and it is no longer controlled by Great Britain and the mean King George.

A committee of five men wrote the statement declaring independense. The committee asked brilliant Thomas Jefferson to write the first draft. He wrote the essay over two week's in June. That's a lot of time to spend writing! It was then revised and edited by Benjamin Franklin and John Adams, the two smartest men around.

The Declaration tells why. The United States is fighting to be its own country and wants to break away from Great Britain, which isn't really so great. It states that the amazing people of the new United States are mad at nasty King George. The Declaration lists all of the horrible things he has done that Americans hate. It also names the rites that the representatives think all people should have. That is such a great idea!

The signers said they believe in the United States of America, and that its people deserve "life, liberty, and the pursuit of happiness."

Writing a Response to Literature

Lesson 1 Introducing a Response to Literature

A response to literature is writing that responds to a prompt, or question, about a specific reading selection.

1. Explain to students that they may be asked to write about a story, passage, or poem when they take a test or during their language arts class. Say: **When you write about something you have read, it is called a response to literature. Often what you will write about comes from a prompt, or question, that follows the story.**

2. Have students read the short story on p. 64. Then read aloud the prompt. Invite volunteers to read aloud the model on p. 65. Then ask: **What is the purpose of this response to literature?** (to explain how Nash contributes more than Elena to the success of the play) Have students write the purpose on the lines provided.

3. Invite students to offer opinions about what makes this a good response to literature. Prompt students by asking: **Does the writer tell who contributed more to the success of the play? Does the writer summarize the story first so you can understand his response? Does the writer provide specific details from the story to support and explain his ideas?** Then explain that students will use the model as they practice the skills needed to write a good response to literature.

Lesson 2 Answering a Prompt

1. Say: **When you see a prompt on a test or during an assignment, your purpose for writing is to answer that prompt. The introduction of your response should clearly answer the prompt and support your answer with a reason.**

2. Direct students to the prompt on p. 64. Ask: **What is this prompt asking us to do?** (to tell who contributes more to the play's success) **What else does the prompt tell us to do?** (to use details from the story) Say: **It's important to read the prompt carefully and understand what you are supposed to do.**

3. Read the prompt aloud and then have a volunteer read aloud the first sentence of the writing model on p. 65. Ask: **Does this introduction answer the prompt?** (yes) **What is the writer going to write about?** (how Nash is prepared and a quick thinker)

4. Direct students to p. 66. Read aloud the directions and point out that all of the prompts on the page refer to "The Play's the Thing."

Name: _____

Response to Literature

Introducing a Response to Literature

Read this short story about a brother and sister.

Reading Selection

Name: _____

Response to Literature

Introducing a Response to Literature

Read this example of a response to literature.

Writing Model

King Nash to the Rescue

In "The Play's the Thing," Nash contributes more than Elena to the play's success because he is prepared and thinks quickly. In the story, Nash and Elena write a play together to perform at a family reunion. Nash wants to rehearse, but Elena does not. Nash ends up practicing by himself. When they put on the play, Elena gets nervous and forgets all her lines. Nash says Elena's first line, and they quickly switch roles. The play is a big hit.

The first reason why Nash contributes more to the play is because he is more prepared to perform than Elena is. Elena does not want to practice and watches TV instead. Nash, on the other hand, practices his lines for hours. When they perform the play, Elena gets nervous and forgets her lines in front of the audience. But Nash is able to switch roles with her because he knows the lines so well.

Nash's quick thinking also helps him save the play. When Elena freezes in front of the audience, Nash realizes she cannot remember her lines. He quickly decides to switch roles, and he and Elena finish the play successfully. If it were not for Nash's quick thinking, the play would have been a disaster.

In the end, Elena and Nash put on a great show that everyone likes. But Nash is the character who helps it succeed the most. He practices by himself to be prepared, and he thinks quickly when Elena forgets her lines.

Writer's Purpose: to explain how Nash contributes more than Elena to the success of the play

© Evan-Moor Corp. • EMC 6015 • Nonfiction Writing   **EXPOSITORY WRITING**   65

Name: _____

Response to Literature

Answering a Prompt

Read each prompt and introduction to a response to literature. Then revise the introduction so that it better answers the prompt.

1. **Prompt:** Do you agree with Elena that Nash worries too much? Explain your answer.
   Introduction: I think that Nash is more worried than Elena. He practices for the play.
   I don't agree that Nash was too worried. He was right to worry because he and Elena needed to practice the play.

2. **Prompt:** How is Nash different from Elena? Explain your answer.
   Introduction: Nash and Elena are very different. She is bossy, but they both like basketball.
   Nash is different from Elena because he works harder than she does.

3. **Prompt:** Did Elena learn a lesson in "The Play's the Thing"? Explain how you know with details from the story.
   Introduction: Elena might have learned a lesson in "The Play's the Thing." She didn't work as hard as Nash did.
   Elena did not learn a lesson because she never changes her behavior. Elena acts the same way at the end as she does at the beginning.

4. **Prompt:** What might have happened if Nash had watched television with Elena instead of rehearsing? Give details that support your answer.
   Introduction: In "The Play's the Thing," Nash didn't want to watch television with Elena. Elena did not practice the play, either.
   If Nash had watched television with Elena instead of rehearsing, neither one of them would have been prepared for the play.

66   **EXPOSITORY WRITING**   Nonfiction Writing • EMC 6015 • © Evan-Moor Corp.

Page 67 / Student Book Page 46

Name: _____

Response to Literature

Summarizing the Text

1. Rewrite this summary of "Goldilocks and the Three Bears" to make it more complete. Add details about the plot and characters.

> A girl goes into a house and eats some food there. She also sits on chairs and sleeps on beds. Then the bears come home.

In "Goldilocks and the Three Bears," a girl goes into
the home of three bears. She sits in their chairs, eats
their food, and goes to sleep in Baby Bear's bed. When
the bears come home, they scare her away.

2. Rewrite this summary of "Jack and the Beanstalk" to remove unnecessary details.

> In "Jack and the Beanstalk," Jack trades his cow for magic beans. The beans are different colors. The beans grow into a huge beanstalk. Jack climbs a very long way. He steals a goose that lays golden eggs from a giant. The giant chases Jack, but Jack chops down the beanstalk. His mother gives him the ax to use.

In "Jack and the Beanstalk," Jack trades his cow for
magic beans. The beans grow into a huge beanstalk. Jack climbs
it and steals a goose that lays golden eggs from a giant.
The giant chases Jack, but Jack chops down the beanstalk.

3. Rewrite this summary of "The Princess and the Pea" to remove personal opinions.

> In "The Princess and the Pea," a queen tests a girl to prove she's a princess. She places a tiny pea under 20 mattresses. That's a lot of mattresses. The girl can't sleep at all. I don't think I would have noticed the pea. The queen says only a real princess would be so sensitive. It's not a very fair test.

In "The Princess and the Pea," a queen tests a girl to
prove she's a princess. She places a tiny pea under 20
mattresses. The girl can't sleep at all. The queen says
only a real princess would be so sensitive.

© Evan-Moor Corp. • EMC 6015 • Nonfiction Writing   **EXPOSITORY WRITING**   **67**

Page 68 / Student Book Page 47

Name: _____

Response to Literature

Marking Up the Text

Read the prompt. Then mark up this adaptation of a fable by H. Berkeley Score. Do the following:

➤ Draw a box around the title.
➤ Underline the main ideas or events.
➤ Draw a star next to details that are important for answering the prompt.

The Argument

One day, Elephant and Crocodile stood by a river and argued about who was the better animal.

"Look how tall I am," said Elephant. "I can tear a tree from the ground with my trunk."

"Size isn't everything," replied Crocodile. "I am a fast and silent swimmer and can see in the muddiest wake."

As they continued fighting, Lion happened to pass by.

"Stop that at once," said Lion. "Tell me the reason for your argument."

"We must know which of us is the better animal!" they both cried at once.

"I can help," said Lion. He pointed to a shiny spot above a wall that stood on the other side of the river. "Do you see the steel helmet on the top of that wall? Bring it to me, and I shall then be able to decide which of you is better."

Crocodile, being so used to the water, dove into the river and reached the opposite ★ bank first. Soon he was standing beside the wall, but he could not reach the helmet. Elephant took his time crossing the river. He then extended his long trunk and reached the helmet quite easily. ★

The two animals then made their way back across the river. Elephant was anxious to keep up with Crocodile. Not watching where he was stepping, Elephant stumbled and dropped the helmet. Crocodile noticed and dove below the water, bringing the ★ helmet up in his fierce jaws. They made it to the bank, and Crocodile laid the helmet at Lion's feet. Lion spoke to Elephant first.

"Because of your size and trunk, you were able to reach the helmet. But then you lost it and couldn't get it back. And you," said Lion, turning to Crocodile. "Although you were unable to reach the helmet, you saved it after Elephant dropped it. You are both special in your own way. Neither is better than the other." ★

Prompt: What lesson do Elephant and Crocodile learn in this fable? Use details to support your answer.

68   **EXPOSITORY WRITING**   Nonfiction Writing • EMC 6015 • © Evan-Moor Corp.

---

5. Say: **Sometimes you can answer the prompt in one sentence, and sometimes you may need to use multiple sentences. What matters most is that your introduction clearly answers the prompt.** Complete the first item with students. Then have them complete the activity in pairs or small groups. Invite students to share their responses.

Lesson 3   Summarizing the Text

1. Explain that a response to literature should briefly summarize the plot or most important details of the reading selection in the first paragraph. Say: **In order for readers to understand your response to literature, they need to understand the story that you are writing about. So, your response should include a short summary of the story.**

2. Ask volunteers to identify the plot summary in "King Nash to the Rescue." (paragraph 1) Point out that it summarizes the entire plot of the selection and contains the most important details. Say: **When you write a summary, do not copy sentences directly from the reading selection, do not include personal opinions, and avoid unnecessary details.**

3. Read aloud the directions for the first item on p. 67. Help students recall important details from "Goldilocks and the Three Bears" that should be included in the summary. (e.g., whose bed Goldilocks sleeps in) Have students complete the activity in pairs or small groups.

Lesson 4   Marking Up the Text

1. Say: **Marking up a reading selection will help you find information to include in your response.** Read aloud the directions for marking up a story on p. 68. Then direct students to the "The Play's the Thing" on p. 64. Read the prompt aloud and ask: **What is this prompt asking us to write about?** (whether Nash or Elena contributed more to the play's success) Say: **Let's look for instances where Nash and Elena contribute to the play's success.** Help students find details from the story that tell about the characters. Explain that by marking up a selection, students can quickly find details to use in their responses.

2. Direct students to p. 68 and read aloud the directions and the prompt. Ask: **What is this prompt telling us to do?** (to write about the lesson that Elephant and Crocodile learn) Say: **As you read, look for details about the lesson they learn.**

3. Have students work independently to mark up the story. Ask volunteers to tell what details they drew stars next to and to explain why.

➤ **Extend the Lesson:** Have students mark up a prompt and reading selection from their reading textbook or from a standardized test.

Lesson 5 Using Details from the Story

1. Inform students that it is important to use specific details from the reading selection when they respond to a prompt. Say: **Those details will support your ideas and help your readers understand those ideas.**

2. Direct students to "King Nash to the Rescue." Say: **This writer gives us two reasons that Nash contributed more to the play's success—his preparation and his quick thinking. The writer supports these claims with specific details, such as how long Nash practiced and what Elena did instead.** Have students identify the details that demonstrate Nash's quick thinking. (When Nash realized Elena did not know her lines, he quickly switched roles.)

3. Direct students to p. 69. Read aloud the directions and have students complete the activity in pairs. Review the answers as a class.

Lesson 6 Reviewing a Response to Literature

1. Review the qualities of a good response to literature: a clear topic sentence that answers the prompt, a short summary of the reading selection, and specific details from the story.

2. Have students read and annotate "Why the Raven's Feathers Are Black" and its prompt on p. 70 independently. Remind them to follow the steps listed on p. 68 for marking up the text.

3. Have students read the response to literature on p. 71 and discuss what can be improved. For example, point out that this response has no topic sentence. Also, tell students to correct any grammar, punctuation, and spelling errors in the draft.

4. Have students revise the response to literature independently on a separate sheet of paper. Remind them that there are many ways to improve the draft. Also remind them to proofread their revisions and check for errors.

5. Invite students to share their revised responses.

Page 69 / Student Book Page 48

Pp. 70–71 and Sample Revision / Student Book pp. 49–50

Introducing a Response to Literature

Read this short story about a brother and sister.

Reading Selection

The Play's the Thing

"You worry too much," Elena said to her brother, Nash. "We don't need to rehearse. Let's play basketball."

Nash hated to disagree with his sister, so he followed Elena outside. Normally they were a good match for one another, but today Elena beat him easily. He couldn't concentrate because he was thinking about the play that he and Elena were performing at the family reunion tomorrow.

The play was Elena's idea. She always came up with fun ideas, and they had a great time writing the play together. It was about a king and a queen who plan to take over the world. Elena thought up a lot of funny lines, especially for the queen, who liked to boss the king around. The king mostly just said "yes" or "no."

After dinner, Nash tried to convince Elena to rehearse the play, but she wanted to watch TV. "Don't be a pest," she said. "We already wrote a terrific play."

Nash decided to practice by himself. He went over the lines for hours. By the time he went to bed, he felt as confident as Elena.

More than 100 relatives and friends showed up at the reunion. At 5:00 P.M., Elena announced that she and Nash had a surprise. They quickly put on their costumes and got ready.

All eyes were on Nash and Elena as they came through the door. The first line was supposed to be Elena's, but Nash saw something in her eyes that he had never seen before—Elena was scared! She was frozen stiff and couldn't remember her lines.

Nash jumped in and said his sister's first line, much to her relief. Nash caught Elena's attention and nodded as he started saying her lines. Elena nodded back. Since Nash knew all of the lines, it was easy for him to switch parts. The play became about a bossy king who liked to tell the queen what to do. The audience loved watching Elena play the shy queen because it was so different from her true personality.

After the play, Nash was worried that his sister might be angry with him for taking her role, but she was all smiles. "Thanks, King Nash," she said. "You really saved us. Maybe I should listen to you more often."

"Yes, you should, Queen Elena," he said. "Now let's go eat."

"Nah," said Elena, grabbing a basketball. "Let's play a quick game first."

Prompt: Who contributes more to the play's success, Elena or Nash? Use details from the story to support your answer.

Introducing a Response to Literature

Read this example of a response to literature.

Writing Model

King Nash to the Rescue

In "The Play's the Thing," Nash contributes more than Elena to the play's success because he is prepared and thinks quickly. In the story, Nash and Elena write a play together to perform at a family reunion. Nash wants to rehearse, but Elena does not. Nash ends up practicing by himself. When they put on the play, Elena gets nervous and forgets all her lines. Nash says Elena's first line, and they quickly switch roles. The play is a big hit.

The first reason why Nash contributes more to the play is because he is more prepared to perform than Elena is. Elena does not want to practice and watches TV instead. Nash, on the other hand, practices his lines for hours. When they perform the play, Elena gets nervous and forgets her lines in front of the audience. But Nash is able to switch roles with her because he knows the lines so well.

Nash's quick thinking also helps him save the play. When Elena freezes in front of the audience, Nash realizes she cannot remember her lines. He quickly decides to switch roles, and he and Elena finish the play successfully. If it were not for Nash's quick thinking, the play would have been a disaster.

In the end, Elena and Nash put on a great show that everyone likes. But Nash is the character who helps it succeed the most. He practices by himself to be prepared, and he thinks quickly when Elena forgets her lines.

Writer's Purpose: _____

_____

Answering a Prompt

Read each prompt and introduction to a response to literature. Then revise the introduction so that it better answers the prompt.

1. **Prompt:** Do you agree with Elena that Nash worries too much? Explain your answer.

   Introduction: I think that Nash is more worried than Elena. He practices for the play.

   _____

   _____

2. **Prompt:** How is Nash different from Elena? Explain your answer.

   Introduction: Nash and Elena are very different. She is bossy, but they both like basketball.

   _____

   _____

3. **Prompt:** Did Elena learn a lesson in "The Play's the Thing"? Explain how you know with details from the story.

   Introduction: Elena might have learned a lesson in "The Play's the Thing." She didn't work as hard as Nash did.

   _____

   _____

4. **Prompt:** What might have happened if Nash had watched television with Elena instead of rehearsing? Give details that support your answer.

   Introduction: In "The Play's the Thing," Nash didn't want to watch television with Elena. Elena did not practice the play, either.

   _____

   _____

Summarizing the Text

1. Rewrite this summary of "Goldilocks and the Three Bears" to make it more complete. Add details about the plot and characters.

   A girl goes into a house and eats some food there. She also sits on chairs and sleeps on beds. Then the bears come home.

   _____

   _____

   _____

   _____

2. Rewrite this summary of "Jack and the Beanstalk" to remove unnecessary details.

   In "Jack and the Beanstalk," Jack trades his cow for magic beans. The beans are different colors. The beans grow into a huge beanstalk. Jack climbs a very long way. He steals a goose that lays golden eggs from a giant. The giant chases Jack, but Jack chops down the beanstalk. His mother gives him the ax to use.

   _____

   _____

   _____

   _____

3. Rewrite this summary of "The Princess and the Pea" to remove personal opinions.

   In "The Princess and the Pea," a queen tests a girl to prove she's a princess. She places a tiny pea under 20 mattresses. That's a lot of mattresses. The girl can't sleep at all. I don't think I would have noticed the pea. The queen says only a real princess would be so sensitive. It's not a very fair test.

   _____

   _____

   _____

   _____

Marking Up the Text

Read the prompt. Then mark up this adaptation of a fable by H. Berkeley Score.
Do the following:

➤ Draw a box around the title.
➤ Underline the main ideas or events.
➤ Draw a star next to details that are important for answering the prompt.

The Argument

One day, Elephant and Crocodile stood by a river and argued about who was the better animal.

"Look how tall I am," said Elephant. "I can tear a tree from the ground with my trunk."

"Size isn't everything," replied Crocodile. "I am a fast and silent swimmer and can see in the muddiest wake."

As they continued fighting, Lion happened to pass by.

"Stop that at once," said Lion. "Tell me the reason for your argument."

"We must know which of us is the better animal!" they both cried at once.

"I can help," said Lion. He pointed to a shiny spot above a wall that stood on the other side of the river. "Do you see the steel helmet on the top of that wall? Bring it to me, and I shall then be able to decide which of you is better."

Crocodile, being so used to the water, dove into the river and reached the opposite bank first. Soon he was standing beside the wall, but he could not reach the helmet. Elephant took his time crossing the river. He then extended his long trunk and reached the helmet quite easily.

The two animals then made their way back across the river. Elephant was anxious to keep up with Crocodile. Not watching where he was stepping, Elephant stumbled and dropped the helmet. Crocodile noticed and dove below the water, bringing the helmet up in his fierce jaws. They made it to the bank, and Crocodile laid the helmet at Lion's feet. Lion spoke to Elephant first.

"Because of your size and trunk, you were able to reach the helmet. But then you lost it and couldn't get it back. And you," said Lion, turning to Crocodile. "Although you were unable to reach the helmet, you saved it after Elephant dropped it. You are both special in your own way. Neither is better than the other."

Prompt: What lesson do Elephant and Crocodile learn in this fable?
Use details to support your answer.

Name: _____

Using Details from the Story

Read the story. Then complete the sentences with details from the story.

Jamie was tired. She had been on her feet for hours. Her mom owned a small but busy restaurant in town. Two of her mom's employees had called in sick that morning. There was a big festival in the city park that day, and Jamie had wanted to go. But her mom had asked her to help at the restaurant.

All Jamie wanted to do was sit down for a while. Instead, she hurried around the restaurant, taking orders and refilling coffee cups. As soon as one table was cleared, a new set of customers walked in. The customers just kept coming! That meant more orders and more coffee.

"Order up!" called the cook from the kitchen. Jamie stared into the kitchen, thinking about all the food stalls at the festival. Cooks there were preparing special foods from around the world. Jamie imagined the delicious smells of new and exotic foods.

"Hurry, Jamie!" the cook called, catching Jamie lost in thought.

"I'm coming," Jamie grumbled. But her mom had already picked up the plates of hot food from the counter and delivered them to a table by the window.

"Wake up, Jamie," her mom said. "I know you don't want to be here, but I need your help."

1. Jamie's mom needed help because _____

_____.

2. Jamie worked hard by _____

_____.

3. Jamie was scolded because _____

_____.

4. Jamie was daydreaming about _____

_____.

Reviewing a Response to Literature

Read and annotate this short story and prompt. The story is adapted from one by Florence Holbrook.

Reading Selection

Why the Raven's Feathers Are Black

Long, long ago, the raven's feathers were as blue as the sky. He was beautiful, but the other birds did not like him because he was a thief. He stole all of the shiny things they decorated their nests with. Whenever birds saw the raven coming, they would hide their treasures. Nonetheless, he always found their treasures and took them to his nest.

One morning, the raven heard a little bird singing merrily in a thicket. The little bird's bright yellow feathers gleamed like sunshine in the dark forest.

"I must have that bird's golden feathers," thought the raven. He seized the trembling little thing and took her to his nest.

The yellow bird fluttered and cried, "The raven has caught me! Help, help!"

The other birds happened to be far away, so the only animal that heard her cries was a worm hidden in the bark of a tree.

"I am only a worm," he said to himself. "I cannot do much, but the yellow bird does not deserve to be trapped in the raven's nest. I will do what I can to help her."

When the sun set, the raven went to sleep. Then the worm crawled his way up the tree to the raven's nest and bound the raven's feet together with grass.

"Fly away," whispered the worm as he freed the little yellow bird. "I must teach the raven not to be cruel to other birds."

The little yellow bird flew away, and the worm placed twigs and grass around the bottom of the tree. Then he set it all on fire. Up the great pine tree went the flames, leaping from bough to bough.

"Fire! Fire!" cried the raven. "Come and help me! My nest is on fire!"

The other birds did not come to his rescue.

Soon, the fire burned the grass that held the raven's feet together, and he flew away. He was not hurt, but he no longer had bright blue feathers. The smoke had turned every one of them as black as night.

Prompt: How did the raven's personality cause him to lose his bright blue feathers? Explain your answer.

Reviewing a Response to Literature

Revise this response to literature. Use what you have learned to make it stronger. Rewrite it on a separate sheet of paper.

Focus on:

✓ answering the prompt in a clear topic sentence
✓ summarizing the reading selection
✓ using details from the story to support the topic sentence
✓ correcting grammar, punctuation, and spelling errors

Draft

A Bad Bird

I think the ravens' blue feathers turn to black in the smoke. The raven steals things. It is wrong to steal. A worm teaches him a lessun by tying his feet together and starting a fire. That are dangerous!

The raven, steals bright and shiny objekts from the other birds. Stealing things does not make him popular, as the raven finds out. When he is trapped in the fire, none of the other birds will helped him. They are still angry with him for stealing things.

The raven is also mean. If the raven had not been so mean, he would still have beautiful blue feathers.

The raven loses his blue feathers because of his stealing and crewlty. If the raven, had simply been happy with his own things, and treated others better, he might still be bright blue.

Writing a Research Report

Pages 78–81 / Student Book Pages 52–55

A research report is a report that gives details and facts about a topic and uses information gathered from different sources.

1. Tell students that the purpose of a research report is to give interesting facts about a topic. Say: **Before you write your report, you must research to find information.** Ask: **What are some sources you can use to research information for your report?** (books, magazines, the Internet, etc.)

2. Display "A Viking Voyage" on pp. 78 and 79. Read the first two paragraphs aloud and have students identify details they think the writer found by doing research. (e.g., where Vikings lived and traveled)

3. Have students finish reading the report independently. Then ask: **What is the topic of this research report?** (the Viking exploration of North America) **What is the purpose?** (to give information about the first known Viking exploration of North America) Have students write the purpose on the lines provided.

4. Invite students to offer opinions about what makes this a good research report. Prompt students by asking: **Is there one sentence that tells you the topic of the report? Does each paragraph tell you something new about the topic? Is the report easy to read? Can you tell that the writer did research?**

1. Say: **A research report should have a topic sentence that clearly states the report's topic and purpose.** Have students identify the topic sentence in the introduction of "A Viking Voyage." *(However, many historians believe that a Viking named Leif Erikson was the first European to explore North America.)* Invite students to explain what makes this a good topic sentence. (It tells what the report is about and is clear and specific.)

2. Say: **Each body paragraph should also have a sentence that tells the main idea of that paragraph.** Have students work in pairs to determine the main-idea sentence of each body paragraph of "A Viking Voyage" on p. 78. (1. *The Vikings were people who lived in …*; 2. *Around the year 1000, …*; 3. *Leif and his crew were …*; 4. *The Vikings sailed south, …*; 5. *They finally arrived …*; 6. *In 1960, historians Helge Ingstad and Anne Stine Ingstad …*; 7. *When winter was over, …*)

3. Direct students to p. 82 and have volunteers read each paragraph aloud. Ask: **What is this report about?** (how real Vikings were not like Vikings from stories) Read the directions aloud and guide students through the activity, helping them identify the topic sentence in the first paragraph and brainstorming ways to state the idea of each subsequent paragraph.

Lesson 3 Asking Research Questions

1. Review the purpose of a research report. Then say: **Before you begin researching, you should figure out what you need to know about your topic. One way to do this is to ask questions about your topic.**

2. Say: **Let's think of some questions the writer of "A Viking Voyage" might have asked.** List students' questions on the board. (e.g., How many Vikings sailed to North America? Where did they land? etc.) Then discuss why these are good questions to answer in a report. Say: **Asking questions before you research will give you a purpose for researching. This will help you focus and save time as you gather information for your report.**

3. Have students complete the activity on p. 83 in pairs. Ask pairs to share their completed questions and discuss why the questions are good to include in a research report or how they might be improved.

➤ **Extend the Lesson:** Show students how to use common resources, such as an encyclopedia or online newspaper, to research the answers to their questions.

Lesson 4 Taking Notes

1. Explain the purpose of taking notes. Say: **It is impossible to remember all the information you read when you research, so you must write down the facts that you find from each source.** Remind students that a *source* gives them information. It can be a book, Internet site, magazine, or a person.

2. Direct students to p. 84 and discuss the example with them. Point out the name of the source and the page number on the card. Ask: **Why is it a good idea to write these on your notecards?** (so that you can find the information again if you need to) Tell students that when their source is a magazine, the date of publication should also be noted. For sources from the Internet, the Web site address and date that the site was accessed should be noted as well.

Page 82 / Student Book Page 56

Name: _____

Research Report

Writing a Topic Sentence and Main-Idea Sentences

Read these paragraphs from a research report. For the first paragraph, write a topic sentence to tell about the topic of the entire report. For each remaining paragraph, write a sentence to tell that paragraph's main idea.

When most people think of Vikings, they probably think of wild men with long beards and fur cloaks who sailed around and fur cloaks who sailed around and fought everyone they met. But people who study Vikings have discovered many interesting things about them. These discoveries do not match the popular stories about Vikings.

Many ideas that people have about Vikings are not true.

Because the Vikings did not leave behind a good written record, much of what we know about them comes from stories by people who lived during the same time. And some of these stories came from people who had been attacked by Vikings. In their stories, the Vikings were described as evil invaders. Experts believe some of these stories are not trustworthy.

People who disliked Vikings told untrue stories about them.

Stories describe Vikings as hairy men who wore horned helmets and swung huge axes. However, all of the Viking helmets that have been discovered look like normal helmets from that time, and most of the Viking weapons that have been discovered are spears. Vikings also did not have long hair or braided beards. In fact, some hairstyles at that time were even weirder! In *Historical Haircuts*, Nancy Weiss writes, "Around the 10th century, it was not unusual to see people in Europe who let the hair on the front half of their head grow long while they shaved the back half bare."

Vikings did not look like how they were described in stories.

Many stories of Vikings tell about how cruel and violent they were. It is true that the Vikings did attack villages and ships as they explored. However, other groups of explorers did this as well. Vikings were no more cruel or violent than other groups at that time. And many Viking explorers also traded peacefully with other people in Europe.

Vikings were not as cruel or violent as some stories say.

82 EXPOSITORY WRITING — Nonfiction Writing • EMC 6015 • © Evan-Moor Corp.

Page 83 / Student Book Page 57

Name: _____

Research Report

Asking Research Questions

Write three questions that would be important to answer in a research report about each topic.

1. **Topic:** the history of telephones

   Who invented the telephone?

   How did the first phone work?

   When were cell phones invented?

   Why do some phones have cords?

2. **Topic:** volcanoes

   What causes an eruption?

   What is lava made of?

   Which volcano is the biggest in the world?

   Is there any way to predict when a volcano is going to erupt?

3. **Topic:** fossils

   How old is the oldest fossil?

   How are fossils formed?

   Can you find a fossil in any kind of rock?

   How do scientists figure out how old a fossil is?

4. **Topic:** pirates in North and South America

   When did most pirates live?

   Who are some famous pirates?

   Why did people become pirates?

   Are there any pirates in the Americas today?

© Evan-Moor Corp. • EMC 6015 • Nonfiction Writing — EXPOSITORY WRITING **83**

Page 84 / Student Book Page 58

Name: _____

Research Report

Taking Notes

Read each source. Write the name of the source at the top of each card. Then write at least two notes about what the source says.

Example

Source: *Encyclopedia Informatic*, p. 91

Vinland Vinland was the name that the Vikings gave to the island now called Newfoundland. The Vikings spent the winter in a camp there. People have found Viking remains in Vinland.

Encyclopedia Informatic, p. 91
• Vinland is now Newfoundland.
• The Vikings spent winter there.

1. **Source:** *Canadian Geographer*, p. 72

In 1960, Helge Ingstad and Anne Stine Ingstad discovered Norse ruins in L'Anse aux Meadows, located in Newfoundland, Canada. Their discovery was of an old settlement and some Viking tools. This discovery proved that the Vikings visited America 1,000 years ago.

Canadian Geographer, p. 72
• In 1960, Helge Ingstad and Anne Stine Ingstad found ruins in L'Anse aux Meadows, Newfoundland, Canada.
• They discovered Viking tools.
• The discovery proves that Vikings visited North America.

2. **Source:** History4Kids.org

Historians have long argued about the name that Leif Erikson gave to Vinland. The word means a "fertile area full of grapes or pastures." But neither grapevines nor good pastures are commonly found in that area. So what are we to make of the name? Leif may have exaggerated Vinland's beauty and natural resources in order to make it sound appealing to settlers. In other words, the name was likely an early example of false advertising!

History4Kids.org
• Vinland means "a fertile area full of grapes or pastures."
• Vinland has few grapevines or pastures.
• The name Vinland was likely "false advertising" to make the land sound more appealing to settlers.

84 EXPOSITORY WRITING   Nonfiction Writing • EMC 6015 • © Evan-Moor Corp.

Page 85 / Student Book Page 59

Name: _____

Research Report

Writing an Outline

Use the notes on the notecards to complete the outline.

History Just for Kids, pp. 12–16
• Sagas were first told aloud.
• Some sagas were written down hundreds of years later.
• *The Greenland Saga* tells about Leif Erikson's voyage to Vinland.
• In *The Saga of Erik the Red*, a Viking named Thorfinn lands at Vinland, not Leif.

VikingFacts.com
• A saga is a poem or song that tells about an event from history.
• Sagas often have exaggerated details.
• Some details are completely made up.
• Sagas about the same events have different characters and details.
• Even with different details, most sagas are probably about true events.

I. Most of the information about Viking history comes from sagas.
  A. A saga is a poem or song about an event in history.
  B. Sagas were written down years after first being told.
  C. Some details were made up by people telling the saga.
  D. Other details from sagas were exaggerated.

II. The sagas about the Viking voyage to North America tell the story differently.
  A. They have different plots, details, and characters.
  B. The Greenland Saga tells how Leif sailed to Vinland.
  C. The Saga of Erik the Red says a Viking named Thorfinn landed at Vinland, not Leif.
  D. Even though the sagas have different details, they are both probably about a true event.

© Evan-Moor Corp. • EMC 6015 • Nonfiction Writing   EXPOSITORY WRITING 85

---

3. Help students understand the different ways of taking notes. Say: **You can take notes in two ways: by paraphrasing or by quoting. When you paraphrase, you write the information in your own words. When you quote, you copy the exact words from the source. It's a good idea to use quotation marks in your notes when you quote information so that you remember that those are someone else's words and not your own.**

4. Have students complete the activity in pairs. Ask pairs to share their answers.

➤ **Extend the Lesson:** Provide each student with a notecard and a source, such as a magazine article or a page printed from a Web site. Then have students take notes from those sources.

Lesson 5 Writing an Outline

1. Direct students to the outline model on p. 81. Explain that the purpose of writing an outline is to organize information to make it easier to write a report with well-developed paragraphs. Say: **Writing an outline will also help you see if you are missing any information from your notes.** Then point out the structure of the outline. Say: **Roman numerals are used with main ideas, and capital letters are for detail sentences that support the main idea.**

2. Have students identify the main-idea sentences and the detail sentences in the outline model. Then help them compare the outline to the model report in order to understand how the outline helped the writer organize the information in the report.

3. Direct students to p. 85 and read the instructions aloud. Then review the information in the notecards to confirm that students understand the content.

4. Have a volunteer read aloud the sentence next to the first Roman numeral. Then say: **Use the notecards to find one detail that tells more about this statement.** (e.g., A saga is a poem or song about an event in history.) Have students complete the activity.

Lesson 6 Using an Outline to Write

1. Direct students to the outline model on p. 81. Say: **When you write your research report, you can refer to your outline to help you organize the details into clear paragraphs that flow naturally.**

2. Use the outline model and the model report on p. 78 to help students see how the main-idea and detail sentences from the outline were incorporated into each paragraph of the report.

3. Read aloud the instructions for the activity on p. 86 and guide students through the activity. Point out that each section of the outline becomes a separate paragraph. Remind students to write their paragraphs so that the sentences flow naturally together and are not just copied directly from the outline.

Lesson 7 Quoting and Paraphrasing

1. Remind students that a research report is made up of factual information about a topic. Say: **The information that you include in a research report comes from many sources. When you write, you should explain that information in your own words. This is called paraphrasing.** Direct students to the fifth paragraph of "A Viking Voyage" on p. 78 and have a volunteer read it aloud. Ask: **What information from the article by Kim Wehru did the writer paraphrase?** (the information about where Markland probably was and why it was important to other Vikings) **How do you know?** (The writer mentions the article where she found the information.)

2. Say: **Sometimes, instead of paraphrasing, it is better to share someone's opinion or explain a piece of interesting information exactly as that person wrote it. Remember to put the words in quotation marks and tell who wrote them or where they came from.**

3. Have students find the quotations in "A Viking Voyage." (paragraph 3: *According to VikingFacts.com, …;* paragraph 7: *Barbara Stoll writes, …*) If necessary, clarify that the writer used quotation marks in other places in the report to tell what the Viking names for places meant, but these are not quotes from a source.

4. Have students complete the activities on p. 87 independently or in pairs. Ask volunteers to share their revised paragraphs.

Page 86 / Student Book Page 60

Name: _____

Research Report

Using an Outline to Write

Use the information from the outline to complete two paragraphs about Viking sagas. Remember to put the information in your own words so that the sentences flow together.

I. Much of the information about Viking history comes from two ancient stories, or sagas.
   A. A saga is a poem or song about an event in history.
   B. Viking sagas were first told aloud, and then written down many years later.
   C. Some details in sagas were made up by the person telling the saga.
   D. Other details in sagas were exaggerated.

II. The sagas about the trip to North America do not agree on what happened.
   A. They have some differences in the plot, details, and characters.
   B. The Greenland Saga describes Leif's discovery of Vinland.
   C. The Saga of Erik the Red tells that a Viking named Thorfinn landed at Vinland.
   D. Even though the sagas have different details, they are probably about the same event.

Much of what we know about Viking history comes from ancient sagas.

A saga is a poem or song about a true event. Vikings first told their sagas aloud. It was not until many years later that sagas were written down. Not all of the details in the sagas are facts. Some details were exaggerated, and other details were probably made up by the writer.

There are two sagas about the Viking voyage to North America: The Greenland Saga and The Saga of Erik the Red.

The sagas have slightly different plots, details, and characters. The Greenland Saga tells that Leif led the voyage to Vinland. However, The Saga of Erik the Red states that a Viking named Thorfinn is the person who sailed to Vinland. Even though the sagas do not agree on the details, they are both probably about the same event.

86 EXPOSITORY WRITING   Nonfiction Writing • EMC 6015 • © Evan-Moor Corp.

Page 87 / Student Book Page 61

Name: _____

Research Report

Quoting and Paraphrasing

Read this entry from *Viking Encyclopedia*. Then rewrite the paragraph below, using some of the information from the entry. Quote some of the information that is underlined, and paraphrase the information that is double-underlined.

Oseberg ship The Oseberg ship is the best preserved Viking ship ever found. It was discovered in 1903 by a farmer near Oslo, Norway. Viking ships were often used in burials, and this ship contained two female skeletons. One of the women was between 60 and 70 years old, and the other woman was 25 to 30 years old. The ship was also filled with chests, household tools, and the skeletons of animals. The ship itself is made of oak and was constructed around AD 820. Its front and back are decorated with many woodcarvings. The ship was carefully removed from where it was found, and rebuilt. It now sits on display in the Viking Ship Museum in Norway.

The Vikings ruled the seas from the 8th through the 11th centuries. Their ships were silent, light, and fast. They were perfect for trading, raiding, and exploring. Scientists have found many Viking ships. Historians know a lot about them.

The Vikings ruled the seas in the Northern Hemisphere from the 8th through the 11th centuries. Their ships were silent, light, and fast. They were perfect for trading, raiding, and exploring. Historians know a lot about them because archaeologists have found many buried Viking ships. According to Viking Encyclopedia, "The Oseberg ship is the best preserved Viking ship ever found." It was built out of oak around AD 820. A farmer found the ship in 1903 near Norway.

© Evan-Moor Corp. • EMC 6015 • Nonfiction Writing   EXPOSITORY WRITING 87

Writing a Research Report, continued

Page 88 / Student Book Page 62

Name: _____

Research Report

Writing Introductions and Conclusions

Read each paragraph and label it as an introduction or a conclusion. For each introduction, underline the topic sentence. For each conclusion, double-underline the information that leaves the reader with a final thought.

1. introduction

On August 23, AD 79, Pompeii was a busy Italian city and popular place to visit, but by August 26, it had disappeared completely. A volcano had erupted and buried the city in ash. The city became an instant tomb for the people who lived there. Today, the buried city of Pompeii provides people with a look at ancient Roman life.

conclusion

The volcano devastated the people and city of Pompeii. However, historians found a rare gift in the catastrophe. They now have a well-preserved Roman city that has taught modern people about daily life in ancient Rome.

2. conclusion

No one may ever know the reason why the Roanoke Colony disappeared or what happened to its people. There are many guesses about what happened, but historians have not yet found evidence to support any of them. The Lost Colony of Virginia is one of the greatest early mysteries in America's history, and by trying to solve it, we learn more about our past.

introduction

In 1590, an English settler named John White returned to an Early American colony named the Roanoke Colony, in Virginia. He was bringing supplies and aid to the settlers he had left behind three years earlier. But when he arrived at the colony, he found it empty. Everyone had disappeared, and there was nothing left behind to tell where they went. Even 400 years later, no one knows the truth about what happened to those people.

88   EXPOSITORY WRITING   Nonfiction Writing • EMC 6015 • © Evan-Moor Corp.

Lesson 8 Writing Introductions and Conclusions

1. Activate prior knowledge by asking what the purpose of an introduction is. (to clearly introduce the topic and grab the readers' attention)

2. Have students find the topic sentence for "A Viking Voyage" on p. 78. *(However, many …)* Ask: **Does this sentence clearly tell you what the report is about?** (yes) Then, if necessary, help students understand the difference between a topic sentence that tells the main idea of the entire report and the sentences that tell the main idea of each paragraph. (The main-idea sentences support the topic sentence.)

3. Say: **There are many ways to make an introduction interesting. How does the writer make the introduction to this report interesting?** (She gives an interesting piece of trivia about Christopher Columbus and Vikings.) Then have students brainstorm other ways to make an introduction to a report about Vikings interesting. (Use vivid details to describe the voyage, create suspense about some part of the trip, give other facts about Vikings, etc.)

4. Turn students' attention to the conclusion of the report on p. 79. Say: **A good conclusion summarizes the most important information that readers should take away from the report. It should also leave your readers with a final thought.** Read aloud the conclusion of "A Viking Voyage" and ask: **Which sentence sums up important information from the report?** *(Leif Erikson's voyage …)* **What final thought did the writer want to leave you with?** (At least more people are realizing that the true discovery of America was made by Vikings.)

5. Direct students' attention to p. 88 and read the instructions aloud. Guide students through the paragraphs to make sure they understand the content. Then have students complete the activity.

Lesson 9 Listing Sources

1. Direct students to the model bibliography on p. 80. Say: **A research report must include a bibliography, or a list of sources you used. It tells where the information in your report came from.** Ask: **What kinds of sources were used to research "A Viking Voyage"?** (two Web sites, an encyclopedia, a book, and two magazine articles)

---

2. Guide students through the first citation and discuss each part (title of entry, title of the encyclopedia, edition, year printed). Ask: **Why is it unnecessary to include the page number with encyclopedia entries?** (Entries are organized alphabetically, so they are easy to find without page numbers.)

3. Point out that the sources in a bibliography are always listed in alphabetical order by the author's last name or the title of the source. Continue to guide students through the remainder of the bibliography, and have students label the parts of each citation.

4. Have students work in small groups to complete the activity on p. 89. Invite them to refer to their labeled bibliographies to make sure they write each citation correctly, with all the information and in the right order.

➤ **Extend the Lesson:** Have students choose a few sources from the Internet and the library to practice writing bibliographies.

Lesson 10 Reviewing a Research Report

1. Review some of the qualities of a good research report: clear topic sentences, paraphrasing and quoting of information, well-organized details, an introduction and a conclusion, and a bibliography.

2. Point out the partial outline on p. 90 and the excerpt from a book about chocolate. Invite a volunteer to read aloud each one.

3. Have students read "Everyone Loves Chocolate," and discuss what might be improved. For example, ask: **Did this report quote a source?** (no) **Did it include all of the information in the outline?** (no) **What is missing?** (that wealthy Mayans had special cups for chocolate) **That interesting detail would be good to include in the report.** Then ask: **Does the second paragraph have a clear topic sentence?** (no) Also, tell students to correct any grammar, punctuation, and spelling errors in the draft.

4. Have students revise the research report paragraphs independently on a separate sheet of paper. Remind them that there are different ways to improve the draft. Also remind them to proofread their revisions and check for errors.

5. Invite students to share their revised reports.

Page 89 / Student Book Page 63

Name: _____ **Research Report**

Listing Sources

Write a bibliography entry for each source. Remember to use the correct format.

1. Title of article: "Deep Underground"
   Author: Tracy Levant
   Magazine: *Kids Discover*
   Pages: 12–15
   Publication Date: October 2009

   Levant, Tracy. "Deep Underground." Kids Discover.
      October 2009: 12-15.

2. Title of entry: "Viking Sagas"
   Author: Richard Hodde
   Encyclopedia: World of Science Encyclopedia
   Publication Date: 2011

   Hodde, Richard. "Viking Sagas." World of Science
      Encyclopedia. 2011.

3. Title of Web article: "Viking Ships"
   Author: Astrid Mead
   Web site and address: Kids4History.com, <http://kids4history.com/viking_ships>

   Mead, Astrid. "Viking Ships." Kids4History.com
      <http://kids4history.com/viking_ships>

4. Title of book: What If You Were a Viking?
   Author: Jorge Paine
   Publishing Company: History Publishing
   Place of Publication: San Francisco, CA
   Publication Date: 2009

   Paine, Jorge. What If You Were a Viking?
      San Francisco, CA: History Publishing, 2009.

© Evan-Moor Corp. • EMC 6015 • Nonfiction Writing   EXPOSITORY WRITING   89

Page 90 and Sample Revision / Student Book Page 64

Name: _____ **Research Report**

Reviewing a Research Report

Read the partial outline and the short passage about the history of chocolate. Use them to revise...
Think...

Sample Answer

Everyone Loves Chocolate

Did you know that people have loved chocolate for over 2,000 years? Some of the first people to taste chocolate long ago were those of the ancient Mayan Empire.

Chocolate comes from cacao trees, which the Mayans grew in their yards and forests. They picked the cacao bean pods and then roasted them. Next, they ground the cacao beans with chili pepper, water, vanilla, cornmeal, and honey into a paste. Then, according to "The History of Chocolate," the Mayans made a "frothy, bitter, and spicy drink by pouring the mixture back and forth between two jars." And though every Mayan drank this chocolate, only the rich had special cups for their chocolate.

90

© Evan-Moor Corp. • EMC 6015 • Nonfiction Writing   **EXPOSITORY WRITING   77**

Introducing a Research Report

Read this example of a research report.

A Viking Voyage

Every October 12, Americans celebrate Columbus Day in honor of Christopher Columbus, who reached North America in 1492. But Columbus wasn't the first European explorer to visit North America. Vikings were! In fact, Vikings sailed across the Atlantic Ocean almost 500 years before Columbus did. Not every detail of this voyage is known for sure. However, many historians believe that a Viking named Leif Erikson was the first European to explore North America.

The Vikings were people who lived in Sweden, Iceland, Norway, and Denmark between AD 750 and 1100. Many Vikings were craftsmen, farmers, and fishermen, but others were warriors and explorers. They traveled to Russia, Europe, the British Islands, and across the Atlantic Ocean to Iceland and Greenland.

Around the year 1000, Leif Erikson bought a ship and formed a crew to explore the lands west of Greenland. According to VikingFacts.com, "Leif believed that if he sailed farther past Greenland, he could find good places for people to settle." Leif set out with 35 men. Together they reached the northeastern part of North America in the year 1001.

Leif and his crew were not impressed with North America when they first saw it. They had landed in a part of Canada that was full of rocks and glaciers. They named the land Helluland, which means "flat slab land." It was not a good place to spend the winter or to settle, so the Vikings continued to explore.

The Vikings sailed south, eventually reaching a land with plenty of woods and sandy beaches. They named it Markland, which means "forest land." In his article "The Truth About Vikings," Kim Wehru explains that Markland was probably a part of Canada now called Southern Labrador. Wehru believes that although Vikings did not settle in Markland, they did return often to gather wood for building boats.

Introducing a Research Report

Writing Model
continued

Leif's crew left Markland to find a place with more grass and wildlife to hunt. They finally arrived at an island they called Vinland, which means "wine land" or "pasture land." The island was probably Newfoundland, Canada. Here, the Vikings found a beautiful location with plenty of grass, trees, caribou, and salmon. The explorers decided to spend the winter in Vinland.

In 1960, historians Helge Ingstad and Anne Stine Ingstad found the remains of a Viking camp in Newfoundland. They believed this was the place where Leif and his crew spent their winter. In her book *Early North America*, Barbara Stoll writes, "The camp that the Ingstads found proved that Vikings had come to North America 500 years before Columbus did."

When winter was over, the Viking crew returned to Greenland and told others about the new places they had found. Years later, more Vikings sailed to Vinland. They explored the region, traded with natives, hunted walruses for their ivory tusks, and chopped down trees to take back to Greenland. Vikings lived in Vinland for only a short period of time, though. It was too far from their homeland, and it could not be easily defended from natives or other Vikings.

Leif Erikson's voyage to Canada was a tremendous accomplishment, even by today's standards. In fact, in 1964, the United States declared that October 9 was Leif Erikson Day, in honor of the amazing trip. Although Leif Erikson Day is not as widely celebrated as Columbus Day, the holiday helped more people realize who the first European explorers to North America truly were.

Writer's Purpose: _____

_____

Name: _____

Introducing a Research Report

Read this example of a bibliography for "A Viking Voyage."

Bibliography Model

Laine, Rebecca. "Dig the Vikings! New Archaeological Discoveries."
    Canadian Geographer. August 2002: 24–29.

"Leif Erikson." VikingFacts.com. October 8, 2010.
    <http://vikinglives.com/explorers/leiferikson>

"Leif Erikson." *Young Readers' Encyclopedia.* 5th ed. 1999.

Stoll, Barbara. *Early North America.* Chicago: Three Trees Press, 2003.

"Viking Explorers." History4Kids.org. October 9, 2010.
    <http://history4kids.org/vikings/explorers>

Wehru, Kim. "The Truth About Vikings." *History Just for Kids.*
    February 2005: 12–16.

Name: _____

Introducing a Research Report

Read this example of an outline for "A Viking Voyage."

Outline Model

I. The Vikings lived in Sweden, Iceland, Norway, and Denmark.
   A. Vikings were craftsmen, farmers, fishermen, warriors, and explorers.
   B. Vikings reached Russia, Europe, the British Islands, Iceland, and Greenland.

II. Around the year 1000, Leif Erikson sailed to North America.
   A. Leif bought ships and supplies for the trip.
   B. Leif believed land west of Greenland would be good for settlements.
   C. Leif sailed with 35 Vikings and reached North America in 1001.

III. The Vikings landed in North America.
   A. The place they saw first was made up of flat, rocky land and glaciers.
   B. They named it Helluland, or "flat slab land."
   C. The Vikings could not settle for the winter at Helluland.

IV. The Vikings landed at Markland, or "forest land."
   A. Markland had many woods and sandy beaches.
   B. Markland was probably Southern Labrador.
   C. Vikings did not settle Markland, but they traveled there often to gather wood.

V. Leif landed at Vinland, which means "wine land" or "pasture land."
   A. Vinland had grass, trees, caribou, and salmon.
   B. The Vikings spent the winter in Vinland.
   C. Vinland was probably Newfoundland.

VI. Helge Ingstad and Anne Stine Ingstad found a Viking settlement in 1960.
   A. The settlement was probably where Leif and his crew spent the winter.
   B. The discovery proved that Vikings had explored North America 500 years before Columbus did.

VII. The Vikings returned home and told others about the lands they had found.
   A. More Vikings sailed to Vinland.
   B. Vikings traded with natives, hunted walruses, and chopped down trees.
   C. Vikings lived in Vinland for only a few years.
   D. Vinland could not be easily defended.

Writing a Topic Sentence and Main-Idea Sentences

Read these paragraphs from a research report. For the first paragraph, write a topic sentence to tell about the topic of the entire report. For each remaining paragraph, write a sentence to tell that paragraph's main idea.

When most people think of Vikings, they probably think of wild men with long beards and fur cloaks who sailed around and fought everyone they met. But people who study Vikings have discovered many interesting things about them. These discoveries do not match the popular stories about Vikings.

_____

Because the Vikings did not leave behind a good written record, much of what we know about them comes from stories by people who lived during the same time. And some of these stories came from people who had been attacked by Vikings. In their stories, the Vikings were described as evil invaders. Experts believe some of these stories are not trustworthy.

_____

Stories describe Vikings as hairy men who wore horned helmets and swung huge axes. However, all of the Viking helmets that have been discovered look like normal helmets from that time, and most of the Viking weapons that have been discovered are spears. Vikings also did not have long hair or braided beards. In fact, some hairstyles at that time were even weirder! In *Historical Haircuts,* Nancy Weiss writes, "Around the 10th century, it was not unusual to see people in Europe who let the hair on the front half of their head grow long while they shaved the back half bare."

_____

Many stories of Vikings tell about how cruel and violent they were. It is true that the Vikings did attack villages and ships as they explored. However, other groups of explorers did this as well. Vikings were no more cruel or violent than other groups at that time. And many Viking explorers often traded peacefully with other people in Europe.

_____

Asking Research Questions

Write three questions that would be important to answer in a research report about each topic.

1. **Topic:** the history of telephones

_____

_____

_____

_____

2. **Topic:** volcanoes

_____

_____

_____

_____

3. **Topic:** fossils

_____

_____

_____

_____

4. **Topic:** pirates in North and South America

_____

_____

_____

_____

Name: _____

Taking Notes

Read each source. Write the name of the source at the top of each card. Then write at least two notes about what the source says.

Example

Source: *Encyclopedia Informatic*, p. 91

Vinland   Vinland was the name that the Vikings gave to the island now called Newfoundland. The Vikings spent the winter in a camp there. People have found Viking remains in Vinland.

> Encyclopedia Informatic, p. 91
> • Vinland is now Newfoundland.
> • The Vikings spent winter there.

1. **Source:** *Canadian Geographer*, p. 72

In 1960, Helge Ingstad and Anne Stine Ingstad discovered Norse ruins in L'Anse aux Meadows, located in Newfoundland, Canada. Their discovery was of an old settlement and some Viking tools. This discovery proved that the Vikings visited America 1,000 years ago.

2. **Source:** History4Kids.org

Historians have long argued about the name that Leif Erikson gave to Vinland. The word means a "fertile area full of grapes or pastures." But neither grapevines nor good pastures are commonly found in that area. So what are we to make of the name? Leif may have exaggerated Vinland's beauty and natural resources in order to make it sound appealing to settlers. In other words, the name was likely an early example of false advertising!

Name: _____

Writing an Outline

Use the notes on the notecards to complete the outline.

History Just for Kids, pp. 12–16
• Sagas were first told aloud.
• Some sagas were written down hundreds of years later.
• The Greenland Saga tells about Leif Erikson's voyage to Vinland.
• In The Saga of Erik the Red, a Viking named Thorfinn lands at Vinland, not Leif.

VikingFacts.com
• A saga is a poem or song that tells about an event from history.
• Sagas often have exaggerated details.
• Some details are completely made up.
• Sagas about the same events have different characters and details.
• Even with different details, most sagas are probably about true events.

I. Most of the information about Viking history comes from sagas.

    A. _____

    B. _____

    C. _____

    D. _____

II. The sagas about the Viking voyage to North America tell the story differently.

    A. _____

    B. _____

    C. _____

       _____

    D. _____

       _____

Using an Outline to Write

Use the information from the outline to complete two paragraphs about Viking sagas. Remember to put the information in your own words so that the sentences flow together.

I. Much of the information about Viking history comes from two ancient stories, or sagas.
   A. A saga is a poem or song about an event in history.
   B. Viking sagas were first told aloud, and then written down many years later.
   C. Some details in sagas were made up by the person telling the saga.
   D. Other details in sagas were exaggerated.

II. The sagas about the trip to North America do not agree on what happened.
   A. They have some differences in the plot, details, and characters.
   B. The Greenland Saga describes Leif's discovery of Vinland.
   C. The Saga of Erik the Red tells that a Viking named Thorfinn landed at Vinland.
   D. Even though the sagas have different details, they are probably about the same event.

Much of what we know about Viking history comes from ancient sagas.

_____

_____

_____

_____

_____

There are two sagas about the Viking voyage to North America: The Greenland Saga and The Saga of Erik the Red.

_____

_____

_____

_____

_____

Quoting and Paraphrasing

Read this entry from *Viking Encyclopedia*. Then rewrite the paragraph below, using some of the information from the entry. Quote some of the information that is underlined, and paraphrase the information that is double-underlined.

Oseberg ship   The Oseberg ship is the best preserved Viking ship ever found. It was discovered in 1903 by a farmer near Oslo, Norway. Viking ships were often used in burials, and this ship contained two female skeletons. One of the women was between 60 and 70 years old, and the other woman was 25 to 30 years old. The ship was also filled with chests, household tools, and the skeletons of animals. The ship itself is made of oak and was constructed around AD 820. Its front and back are decorated with many woodcarvings. The ship was carefully removed from where it was found, and rebuilt. It now sits on display in the Viking Ship Museum in Norway.

The Vikings ruled the seas from the 8th through the 11th centuries. Their ships were silent, light, and fast. They were perfect for trading, raiding, and exploring. Scientists have found many Viking ships. Historians know a lot about them.

_____

_____

_____

_____

_____

_____

_____

_____

Writing Introductions and Conclusions

Read each paragraph and label it as an introduction or a conclusion. For each introduction, underline the topic sentence. For each conclusion, double-underline the information that leaves the reader with a final thought.

1. _____

On August 23, AD 79, Pompeii was a busy Italian city and popular place to visit, but by August 26, it had disappeared completely. A volcano had erupted and buried the city in ash. The city became an instant tomb for the people who lived there. Today, the buried city of Pompeii provides people with a look at ancient Roman life.

_____

The volcano devastated the people and city of Pompeii. However, historians found a rare gift in the catastrophe. They now have a well-preserved Roman city that has taught modern people about daily life in ancient Rome.

2. _____

No one may ever know the reason why the Roanoke Colony disappeared or what happened to its people. There are many guesses about what happened, but historians have not yet found evidence to support any of them. The Lost Colony of Virginia is one of the greatest early mysteries in America's history, and by trying to solve it, we learn more about our past.

_____

In 1590, an English settler named John White returned to an Early American colony named the Roanoke Colony, in Virginia. He was bringing supplies and aid to the settlers he had left behind three years earlier. But when he arrived at the colony, he found it empty. Everyone had disappeared, and there was nothing left behind to tell where they went. Even 400 years later, no one knows the truth about what happened to those people.

Name: _____

Listing Sources

Write a bibliography entry for each source. Remember to use the correct format.

1. Title of article: "Deep Underground"
   Author: Tracy Levant
   Magazine: *Kids Discover*
   Pages: 12–15
   Publication Date: October 2009

   _____

   _____

2. Title of entry: "Viking Sagas"
   Author: Richard Hodde
   Encyclopedia: *World of Science Encyclopedia*
   Publication Date: 2011

   _____

   _____

3. Title of Web article: "Viking Ships"
   Author: Astrid Mead
   Web site and address: Kids4History.com, <http://kids4history.com/viking_ships>

   _____

   _____

4. Title of book: *What If You Were a Viking?*
   Author: Jorge Paine
   Publishing Company: History Publishing
   Place of Publication: San Francisco, CA
   Publication Date: 2009

   _____

   _____

Name: _____

Reviewing a Research Report

Read the partial outline and the short passage about the history of chocolate. Use them to revise the first two paragraphs of a research report titled "Everyone Loves Chocolate." Think about what you have learned to make the paragraphs stronger.

I. Chocolate was first eaten by ancient Mayans.

    A. The Mayans grew cacao trees.

    B. They picked, roasted, and ground the cacao beans into a paste.

    C. They mixed the paste with chili pepper, water, vanilla, cornmeal, and honey.

    D. Mayans mixed the drink in two jars.

    E. The drink was frothy, bitter, and spicy.

    F. Wealthy Mayans had special cups for drinking chocolate.

The History of Chocolate

The ancient Mayans were among the first people to enjoy chocolate over 2,000 years ago. They got it from cacao trees, which grew in their forests and yards. The people harvested the bean pods, roasted them over a fire, and ground the beans into a paste. Then they added chili pepper, water, vanilla, cornmeal, and honey. Finally, the Mayans poured the mixture back and forth between two jars, creating a frothy, bitter, spicy drink. All Mayans loved chocolate, but only the wealthy had decorated cups used just for chocolate.

Draft

Everyone Loves Chocolate

Everyone likes chocolate. Some of the first people to taste chocolate long ago were those of the ancient Mayan Empire.

The Mayans grew cacao trees in forests and yards. They picked and roasted the bean pods. Then they ground the beans into a paste and mixed in chili pepper, water, vanilla, cornmeal, and honey.

Writing a Persuasive Letter

Lesson 1 Introducing a Persuasive Letter

A persuasive letter is a letter written to persuade a specific person to agree with a certain idea or take a course of action.

1. Tell students that writing a letter is a good way to persuade others. Say: **By writing a letter, you are trying to convince someone specific to agree with an idea you have or to do something you want them to do.**

2. Have students read the model on p. 94. Then have them identify the audience of this letter. (Principal Ny) Ask: **What is the purpose of this letter?** (to persuade Principal Ny to allow a class garden) Have students write the audience and purpose on the lines provided.

3. Invite students to offer opinions about what makes this a good persuasive letter. Prompt students by asking: **Does the beginning of the letter grab your attention? Does Mya clearly state what she wants? Does she provide good reasons for what she wants? Does Mya support her reasons with details?**

Lesson 2 Forming Opinion Statements

1. Explain that a strong persuasive letter should have an *opinion statement*. Say: **An opinion statement is a sentence that specifically tells the writer's position, or what he or she wants the reader to do. It should contain a single main idea.** Have students identify the opinion statement in the model on p. 94. (*To make this happen, all you need to do …*)

2. Write the following statements on the board: *Each lunch period should be 5 minutes longer. I think that each lunch period could be 5 or maybe 10 minutes longer, or maybe only for older students.* Then ask: **Which opinion statement clearly states a position?** (the first one) **Why is the second statement less effective?** (The second opinion statement contains words and phrases such as "I think" and "maybe," which make the writer sound unsure of his opinion.) Point out the phrase "or maybe only for older students." Say: **This writer also included a second idea about the lunch period. It is difficult for the reader to decide what the writer is writing about.**

3. Direct students to p. 95 and read the instructions for Activity A aloud. Have them complete the activity.

4. Complete the first item in Activity B as a class and explain why the revision is better. (It is specific and clearly tells the writer's opinion.) Have students finish the activity independently.

Page 94 / Student Book Page 66

Name: _____   Persuasive Letter

Introducing a Persuasive Letter
Read this example of a persuasive letter.

Writing Model

January 27, 2012

Ruskin Elementary
26 Stratford Ave.
Avon Township, NJ 34817

Dear Principal Ny:

Imagine looking out your window to see students working hard in a beautiful garden and growing their own food. And at the same time, those students are learning about science. It may sound too good to be true, but it isn't. To make this happen, all you need to do is give my class permission to grow a garden at school.

By growing a school garden, we will learn a lot about science. We will study how different kinds of plants grow, what they need to survive, and how insects and animals help or harm plants. We will also learn about nutrition and how food helps our bodies grow and develop.

With a school garden, we will be growing food that we can give to the cafeteria. Other classes will want a garden, too. The school will save money because it will not have to buy as many vegetables.

A local garden store will donate the tools, soil, and seeds we need. Parents have agreed to help us tend the garden. And we promise to work hard and be responsible. If you give us permission to grow a garden, we can learn more about science and save the school money.

Sincerely,

Mya Reynolds

Writer's Audience: __Principal Ny__

Writer's Purpose: __to persuade Principal Ny to allow a class garden__

94 PERSUASIVE WRITING   Nonfiction Writing • EMC 6015 • © Evan-Moor Corp.

Page 95 / Student Book Page 67

Name: _____   Persuasive Letter

Forming Opinion Statements

A. Read each pair of opinion statements. Underline the statement that is clearer and tells the writer's position.

1. Pikeville Elementary should require all students to wear uniforms.
   Uniforms might help Pikeville Elementary students do better in school.

2. I think students would enjoy drinking soft drinks at school like teachers do.
   Students should have the same choices for lunch drinks that teachers have.

3. We need a school nurse who can take care of students who get sick at school.
   It would be nice to have a school nurse who could make kids feel better, but it probably costs too much.

B. Rewrite each opinion statement below to make it clearer or to state an opinion.

1. Some kids say recess should be longer, but other kids probably disagree.
   Recess should be 10 minutes longer.

2. I believe bus rides to school are too noisy and take too long.
   Shorter bus rides make students happier.

3. Students should be allowed to eat snacks in the classroom, but only if they do not make a mess, and only if they share with others, and only if the snacks are healthy.
   Students should be allowed to eat snacks in the classroom.

4. Fifth graders probably won't get into much trouble if they are allowed to go to the restroom without a hall pass.
   Fifth graders are mature enough to go to the restroom without a pass.

© Evan-Moor Corp. • EMC 6015 • Nonfiction Writing   PERSUASIVE WRITING 95

© Evan-Moor Corp. • EMC 6015 • Nonfiction Writing   **PERSUASIVE WRITING 91**

Writing a Persuasive Letter, continued

Name: _____

Persuasive Letter

Including Reasons and Details

A. Check the box next to the reason that best supports the opinion statement.

1. **Opinion statement:** Pikeville Elementary should require students to wear uniforms.
   - ☑ **Reason:** Some students are teased because they cannot afford nice clothes.
   - ☐ **Reason:** I do not like picking out clothes to wear in the morning.

2. **Opinion statement:** Students should be allowed to purchase soft drinks at school.
   - ☑ **Reason:** The money raised from soft drinks could help pay for the music program.
   - ☐ **Reason:** Everyone likes soft drinks.

B. Read each opinion statement and reason. Write a good detail sentence that supports the reason.

> **Example**
>
> **Opinion statement:** The school should install security cameras.
>
> **Reason:** More cameras around the school will make the school safer.
>
> **Detail:** A camera by the bike rack will prevent people from stealing bikes.

1. **Opinion statement:** We need more school buses that have shorter routes.

   Reason: Long bus rides home cut into the time students have between school and sleep.

   Detail: Some students do not have time to do homework.

2. **Opinion statement:** It's important for us to have a school nurse.

   Reason: Because we do not have a school nurse, many students go home just for a headache.

   Detail: A nurse could give students medicine.

3. **Opinion statement:** We should be allowed to go on a trip to the science museum.

   Reason: A field trip to the science museum would let us experience what we are learning about in our science books.

   Detail: We would better remember what we learn.

96 PERSUASIVE WRITING   Nonfiction Writing • EMC 6015 • © Evan-Moor Corp.

Name: _____

Persuasive Letter

Writing Good Leads

A. Write the letter of each lead next to the kind of lead it is.

_d_ 1. Bold statement
_e_ 2. Personal story
_b_ 3. Facts
_a_ 4. Emotional appeal
_c_ 5. Vivid description

a. You don't want your students to get hurt, do you? Then please fix the playground equipment. It is dangerous, and we deserve a better place to play.

b. Playground accidents are the number one cause of injuries at elementary schools.

c. As you walk through the gate, you can see the signs of neglect. Swings hang by one chain, the slide has a hole in it, and the jungle gym is just a pile of metal.

d. The school playground is a disaster area!

e. At recess last Thursday, I ran out to a swing, jumped on, and fell flat on my back. Ouch! The swing was broken, just like everything else on the playground.

B. For each opinion statement, write a strong lead.

1. Our school should require students to wear uniforms.

   Vivid description: Imagine never having to send your students to the office for wearing baggy pants, torn shirts, baseball caps, or other clothing that's against the rules.

2. Fifth graders should be allowed to go to the restroom without a hall pass.

   Bold statement: Stop treating fifth graders like babies!

3. The computer lab should be open to students before and after school hours.

   Emotional appeal: Many students do not have computers at home. Do you want to harm students' grades because they have no way to use a computer for their homework?

© Evan-Moor Corp. • EMC 6015 • Nonfiction Writing   **PERSUASIVE WRITING** 97

Lesson 3 Including Reasons and Details

1. Remind students that in order to persuade someone to do something, they must give strong reasons that support their opinions. Direct students to the model letter on p. 94 and have them circle the two main reasons why Mya wants a class garden. (*We will learn a lot about science. We will be growing our own food.*)

2. Point out that Mya writes about each reason in a separate paragraph. Say: **Each reason is a main idea for the paragraph. The rest of the paragraph gives details to support that reason.** Draw students' attention to the second paragraph. Ask: **What details did Mya use to support her first reason that she will learn about science?** (can study how plants grow and survive, how animals and insects help or harm plants) Have students underline the details and then repeat the process for the second reason.

3. Have students complete Activity A on p. 96, and review the answers. Then guide students through the example for Activity B before students complete the activity. Remind students that there can be many details that support each reason.

➤ **Extend the Lesson:** Distribute letters to the editor from newspapers. Have students circle the reasons and underline the details for each writer's opinion.

Lesson 4 Writing Good Leads

1. Say: **The first sentence or two of your letter is called a lead. Your lead should be interesting so that it makes your readers want to continue reading.**

2. Read aloud the lead in the model. Ask: **What makes this a good lead?** (It includes vivid descriptions and mentions things most principals care about.)

3. Use Activity A on p. 97 to introduce the different types of leads. Say: **A bold statement is a simple, strong announcement of the problem you are writing about. A personal story tells about something that happened to you that is also related to your topic. A lead containing a fact gives information about your topic. An emotional appeal makes your reader feel a certain way, such as being proud of something. A vivid description uses adjectives and precise nouns to paint a mental picture for your reader.** Then have students complete the activity.

---

4. Have students complete Activity B in pairs. Encourage partners to imagine themselves in the situations that are described and to discuss what they might say. Invite volunteers to share their answers.

➤ **Extend the Lesson:** Have students find and identify different types of leads in the letters to the editor they read in the Lesson 3 extension activity. Discuss which leads can or should be improved.

Lesson 5 Organizing a Persuasive Letter

1. Say: **A persuasive letter is like any other letter. It has a certain format and organization.** Use the model to introduce or review the parts of a persuasive letter: date, recipient's address, greeting (e.g., *Dear* or *To whom it may concern* and the name of the recipient), introduction (lead and opinion statement), body (reasons and details), conclusion (wrap-up, restatement of the opinion), closing (e.g., *Sincerely*), and signature. Focus on punctuation, spacing, and indentation as you see fit.

2. Return students' attention to the paragraphs within the model letter on p. 94. Point out the organization of information in the letter by asking students to identify its opinion statement, reasons, and supporting details.

3. Have students complete the activities on p. 98 in pairs. Review the answers as a class.

Lesson 6 Reviewing a Persuasive Letter

1. Review the qualities of a good persuasive letter: a good lead, a strong opinion statement, good reasons and supporting details, and proper format and organization.

2. Have students read the letter on p. 99 and discuss what might be improved. For example, point out that the introduction does not clearly state the problem or the writer's opinion. Also, tell students to correct any grammar, punctuation, and spelling errors in the draft.

3. Have students revise the letter independently on a separate sheet of paper. Remind them that there may be different ways to fix the letter. Also remind them to proofread their revisions and check for errors.

4. Invite students to share their revisions with the class.

Page 98 / Student Book Page 70

Name: _____

Persuasive Letter

Organizing a Persuasive Letter

A. Read the letter. Then label each part of the letter with the correct number from the list.

Letter Parts
1. Address
2. Body
3. Date
4. Closing
5. Greeting
6. Introduction
7. Signature
8. Conclusion

3 January 24, 2012

1 Marian Walker
928 Lone Oak Ave.
Cincinnati, OH 56137

5 Dear Mom,

6 Every day, I come home, go to my room, and play by myself. It's time I had a pet to keep me company. And I think that pet should ★ be a raccoon.

2 (A raccoon is not expensive to care for.) It can be fed our table scraps. It doesn't need much cleaning or grooming. And I would share my room with it.
(Raccoons are really smart.) They like to play games with people. I could teach one to use a litter box. I could even teach it commands, such as "no" and "down."

8 Please don't let me be bored and lonely anymore. I need a friend to play with. Because it is inexpensive and smart, I believe that a raccoon is the perfect pet.

4 Sincerely,
7 Dante Walker

B. Look back at the letter. Draw a star by the opinion statement. Circle the two reasons. Underline the details that the writer gives for each reason.

98 PERSUASIVE WRITING   Nonfiction Writing • EMC 6015 • © Evan-Moor Corp.

Page 99 and Sample Revision / Student Book Page 71

Name: _____

Persuasive Letter

Re...
Revis...
Rew...
Focu...

Sample Answer

December 2, 2012

Bluffton Elementary School
1311 Woodbridge Drive
Bluffton, NC 29967

Dear Principal Scroggins,
    Last year, Bluffton Elementary had the lowest test scores in our school district. I believe there is one clear way to improve those scores. You should begin an after-school tutoring program.
    Sometimes, students need extra practice or help in certain subjects. But teachers do not always have time to meet with each student. If we had tutoring, students could get the help they need. Then students' grades would improve.
    After-school tutoring would also help our standardized test scores to improve. When students know the subjects better through tutoring, then test scores should rise. And higher test scores will help our school.
    People might think that nobody would help run the program or that it would cost too much. But that's not true. Parents and teachers will volunteer to help students, and we can ask businesses to donate money or supplies. People will want to help our school, so please offer after-school tutoring at Bluffton Elementary.

Sincerely,
Jake Ono

Name: _____

Introducing a Persuasive Letter

Read this example of a persuasive letter.

Writing Model

January 27, 2012

Ruskin Elementary
26 Stratford Ave.
Avon Township, NJ 34817

Dear Principal Ny:

Imagine looking out your window to see students working hard in a beautiful garden and growing their own food. And at the same time, those students are learning about science. It may sound too good to be true, but it isn't. To make this happen, all you need to do is give my class permission to grow a garden at school.

By growing a school garden, we will learn a lot about science. We will study how different kinds of plants grow, what they need to survive, and how insects and animals help or harm plants. We will also learn about nutrition and how food helps our bodies grow and develop.

With a school garden, we will be growing food that we can give to the cafeteria. Other classes will want a garden, too. The school will save money because it will not have to buy as many vegetables.

A local garden store will donate the tools, soil, and seeds we need. Parents have agreed to help us tend the garden. And we promise to work hard and be responsible. If you give us permission to grow a garden, we can learn more about science and save the school money.

Sincerely,

Mya Reynolds

Writer's Audience: _____

Writer's Purpose: _____

_____

Forming Opinion Statements

A. Read each pair of opinion statements. Underline the statement that is clearer and tells the writer's position.

1. Pikeville Elementary should require all students to wear uniforms.

   Uniforms might help Pikeville Elementary students do better in school.

2. I think students would enjoy drinking soft drinks at school like teachers do.

   Students should have the same choices for lunch drinks that teachers have.

3. We need a school nurse who can take care of students who get sick at school.

   It would be nice to have a school nurse who could make kids feel better, but it probably costs too much.

B. Rewrite each opinion statement below to make it clearer or to state an opinion.

1. Some kids say recess should be longer, but other kids probably disagree.

   _____

   _____

2. I believe bus rides to school are too noisy and take too long.

   _____

   _____

3. Students should be allowed to eat snacks in the classroom, but only if they do not make a mess, and only if they share with others, and only if the snacks are healthy.

   _____

   _____

4. Fifth graders probably won't get into much trouble if they are allowed to go to the restroom without a hall pass.

   _____

   _____

Including Reasons and Details

A. Check the box next to the reason that best supports the opinion statement.

1. **Opinion statement:** Pikeville Elementary should require students to wear uniforms.

   ☐ **Reason:** Some students are teased because they cannot afford nice clothes.
   ☐ **Reason:** I do not like picking out clothes to wear in the morning.

2. **Opinion statement:** Students should be allowed to purchase soft drinks at school.

   ☐ **Reason:** The money raised from soft drinks could help pay for the music program.
   ☐ **Reason:** Everyone likes soft drinks.

B. Read each opinion statement and reason. Write a good detail sentence that supports the reason.

> **Example**
>
> **Opinion statement:** The school should install security cameras.
>
> **Reason:** More cameras around the school will make the school safer.
>
> **Detail:** _A camera by the bike rack will prevent people from stealing bikes._

1. **Opinion statement:** We need more school buses that have shorter routes.

   Reason: Long bus rides home cut into the time students have between school and sleep.

   Detail: _____

2. **Opinion statement:** It's important for us to have a school nurse.

   Reason: Because we do not have a school nurse, many students go home just for a headache.

   Detail: _____

3. **Opinion statement:** We should be allowed to go on a trip to the science museum.

   Reason: A field trip to the science museum would let us experience what we are learning about in our science books.

   Detail: _____

Writing Good Leads

A. Write the letter of each lead next to the kind of lead it is.

_____ 1. Bold statement

_____ 2. Personal story

_____ 3. Facts

_____ 4. Emotional appeal

_____ 5. Vivid description

a. You don't want your students to get hurt, do you? Then please fix the playground equipment. It is dangerous, and we deserve a better place to play.

b. Playground accidents are the number one cause of injuries at elementary schools.

c. As you walk through the gate, you can see the signs of neglect. Swings hang by one chain, the slide has a hole in it, and the jungle gym is just a pile of metal.

d. The school playground is a disaster area!

e. At recess last Thursday, I ran out to a swing, jumped on, and fell flat on my back. Ouch! The swing was broken, just like everything else on the playground.

B. For each opinion statement, write a strong lead.

1. Our school should require students to wear uniforms.

   Vivid description: _____

   _____

   _____

2. Fifth graders should be allowed to go to the restroom without a hall pass.

   Bold statement: _____

   _____

3. The computer lab should be open to students before and after school hours.

   Emotional appeal: _____

   _____

   _____

Name: _____

Organizing a Persuasive Letter

A. Read the letter. Then label each part of the letter with the correct number from the list.

Letter Parts
1. Address
2. Body
3. Date
4. Closing
5. Greeting
6. Introduction
7. Signature
8. Conclusion

_____ January 24, 2012

_____ Marian Walker
928 Lone Oak Ave.
Cincinnati, OH 56137

_____ Dear Mom,

Every day, I come home, go to my room, and play by myself. It's time I had a pet to keep me company. And I think that pet should be a raccoon.

A raccoon is not expensive to care for. It can be fed our table scraps. It doesn't need much cleaning or grooming. And I would share my room with it.

Raccoons are really smart. They like to play games with people. I could teach one to use a litter box. I could even teach it commands, such as "no" and "down."

Please don't let me be bored and lonely anymore. I need a friend to play with. Because it is inexpensive and smart, I believe that a raccoon is the perfect pet.

_____ Sincerely,
_____ *Dante Walker*

B. Look back at the letter. Draw a star by the opinion statement. Circle the two reasons. Underline the details that the writer gives for each reason.

Nonfiction Writing • EMC 6015 • © Evan-Moor Corp.

Reviewing a Persuasive Letter

Revise this persuasive letter. Use what you have learned to make it stronger.
Rewrite the letter on a separate sheet of paper.

Focus on:
- ✓ writing a good lead
- ✓ writing an opinion statement that tells the opinion, or position, and the main idea
- ✓ including reasons and details that support the opinion
- ✓ properly organizing the letter
- ✓ correcting grammar, punctuation, and spelling errors

Draft

December 2, 2012

Bluffton Elementary School
1311 Woodbridge Drive
Bluffton, NC 29967

Principal Scroggins:

I do not think that Bluffton Elementary had good test scores last year. So I was wundering if maybe you should think about starting a free after-school tutoring program, or maybe some other thing to help us score better.

Students want to do better, but they cannot get all the help they need in class. If our school had a tutoring program. Students could get better grades and test scores.

I understanded that a tutoring program could costs a lot. But I am sure that business in the community would dohnate money once they know how important the program is. So please offer free after-school tutoring, that would help all students in our school, be successful.

Jake Ono

Writing a Persuasive Essay

Page 103 / Student Book Page 73

Page 104 / Student Book Page 74

Lesson 1 Introducing a Persuasive Essay

A persuasive essay is an essay written to persuade others to agree with the writer or to take a specific action.

1. Have students read the model on p. 103. When they have finished, ask: **What is the purpose of this essay?** (to persuade readers that students should watch less TV) Have students write the purpose on the lines provided.

2. Invite students to offer opinions about what makes this a good persuasive essay. Prompt by asking: **Does the writer clearly state his opinion about how much television kids should watch? Does he support his reasons with examples? Does he address possible disagreements with his opinion? What specific action does he want readers to take?**

Lesson 2 Writing an Opinion Statement

1. Review the purpose of a persuasive essay. Then say: **In a persuasive essay, a writer uses the topic sentence to make his or her opinion about the topic clear. This sentence is called an opinion statement.**

2. Have students identify the opinion statement in "Turn Off the TV." *(Watching TV harms students' ability to learn and stay healthy, so students should watch less television each day.)* Point out that it contains both a topic or main idea (watching television harms students' learning and health) and the writer's opinion about it (students should watch less television).

3. Ask volunteers to read aloud the paragraphs in Activity A on p. 104. As a class, discuss why each underlined opinion statement needs to be improved. (1. vague topic, 2. states the topic but not an opinion) Have students revise the statements.

4. Have students complete Activity B independently. Then pair students and have partners check each other's statements to make sure they express an opinion and contain a single main idea. Invite volunteers to share their statements.

➤ **Extend the Lesson:** Brainstorm with students a list of possible persuasive essay topics. Then have them choose one and write an opinion statement for it.

Lesson 3 Including Reasons and Examples

1. Say: **Once you write a clear opinion statement, you must then write reasons why your readers should agree with your opinion. The reasons should be related to your opinion and should be supported by specific examples.**

2. Draw the organizer from p. 105 on the board. Have students identify the first reason and its examples in "Turn Off the TV" and write them in the organizer. (Reason: trouble at school. Examples: lower grades, behavior problems, trouble concentrating, less time for homework and reading) Discuss how the reason is related to the writer's opinion and how each example supports the reasons.

3. Have students complete Activity A on p. 105 in pairs. Review the answers as a class, making sure students' reasons support the opinion statement and that the examples support the reasons.

4. Have students complete Activity B independently. Remind students to write sentences that flow together naturally.

➤ **Extend the Lesson:** Have students draw an organizer like the one on p. 105. Then have them complete it with a reason and examples for the opinion statement they wrote in the Lesson 2 extension activity.

Lesson 4 Including an Opposing Reason and a Response

1. Say: **When you write a persuasive essay, you should think of a reason that someone might disagree with your opinion. Then you can respond to that opposing reason.**

2. Have students identify the opposing reason and response in the writing model on p. 103. (some shows are educational; kids watching them are still sitting in front of the TV) Ask students to explain how the response makes the essay more persuasive. (It shows that the writer has thought about a reason why people might disagree and offers a good response to that reason.)

3. Discuss the example on p. 106 with students. Then have them complete the activity in pairs or small groups. Invite students to share their answers.

➤ **Extend the Lesson:** Have students write an opposing argument and response for the opinion statement they wrote in the Lesson 2 extension activity.

Page 105 / Student Book Page 75

Name: _____   Persuasive Essay

Including Reasons and Examples

A. Fill in the graphic organizer with a reason and three examples that support the opinion statement.

Opinion statement: Teachers should not assign homework on Fridays.

> Reason: Kids need time to relax and play on weekends.
>
> Example 1: Kids need to spend time with members of their families.
>
> Example 2: Kids need more time to exercise and play outside.
>
> Example 3: Many students take music lessons or play sports on the weekends.

B. Use the information from the organizer in Activity A to write a persuasive paragraph.

During the weekends, kids need time to relax and play instead of doing homework. They need to spend quality time with their families. They also need to play outside and run around so they can get more exercise and fresh air. And students need time on the weekends to develop other interests, such as playing music or sports.

© Evan-Moor Corp. • EMC 6015 • Nonfiction Writing   **PERSUASIVE WRITING   105**

Page 106 / Student Book Page 76

Name: _____   Persuasive Essay

Including an Opposing Reason and a Response

Read each opinion statement. Then write a possible reason against it and a response to that reason.

> **Example**
> Lakeland Elementary should switch to energy-saving light bulbs.
> **Reason against:** The switch would cost a lot of money.
> **Response:** The school would save more money over time.

1. Students should have to do volunteer work in their community.
   Reason against: Students are already too busy outside of school.
   Response: Students would learn to spend time doing more important things.

2. The computer lab should be open to students for an hour before and after school.
   Reason against: The school will have to pay for a lab monitor.
   Response: Teachers could volunteer to monitor once a month.

3. Students should be required to sell fruit instead of candy to raise money for the school.
   Reason against: Kids do not like fruit as much as candy.
   Response: Fruit is healthier, so parents will buy more of it.

4. Ashton Elementary should start a food bank for its students and their families.
   Reason against: The school has no extra room to store the food.
   Response: The closet by the music room is empty.

5. The cafeteria should lower the price of lunches.
   Reason against: The school would lose too much money.
   Response: The school can ask for donations from the community.

106   PERSUASIVE WRITING   Nonfiction Writing • EMC 6015 • © Evan-Moor Corp.

Writing a Persuasive Essay, continued

Page 107 / Student Book Page 77

Name: _____

Persuasive Essay

Writing Action Statements

A. Revise each action statement.

Example

> **Problem:** The cafeteria never changes its menu.
> **Action statement:** Get the cafeteria to serve ice cream.
> **Revised statement:** Ask the cafeteria manager to serve a new meal once a week.

1. **Problem:** There are too many plastic bags in landfills.
   Action statement: Never go to a store again.
   Revised statement: Take reusable cloth bags every time you shop.

2. **Problem:** Educational video games are not used enough in school.
   Action statement: Play more video games at home.
   Revised statement: Suggest a game to your teacher that might help students with their academic skills.

3. **Problem:** The school has canceled all field trips because of lack of money.
   Action statement: Think about what you can do.
   Revised statement: Ask adults to donate to a field trip fund.

B. Write an action statement for each problem.

1. **Problem:** The library was flooded, and many books were ruined.
   Action statement: Donate some of your books to the library.

2. **Problem:** The public school does not offer swim lessons.
   Action statement: Write a letter to the pool director asking for swim lessons.

© Evan-Moor Corp. • EMC 6015 • Nonfiction Writing   **PERSUASIVE WRITING** 107

Page 108 and Sample Revision / Student Book Page 78

Name: _____

Persuasive Essay

Reviewing a Persuasive Essay

Revise
strong

Focus

Sample Answer

Don't Give Up on Sports

Millions of people play sports. They play soccer, football, basketball, and baseball. But there are millions of other people out there who do not play sports because they do not like team sports. However, people should try a sport that does not require being on a team before they give up on sports altogether.

Sports that do not require playing on a team can help people get the exercise they need. For example, cycling and hiking strengthen the legs. Swimming and gymnastics develop back muscles. And martial arts and dance keep people flexible.

Sports that do not have teams still bring people together. Kids and adults of all ages can participate at the same time. Even though there are no teams, people are sure to make new friends that play their sport.

Some people may argue that sports without teams are not exciting because you do not play a game. But you can still compete in individual sports. Swim meets and bike races are as exciting as football or baseball games.

People should never think they cannot be athletes. Most likely, they just have not found the right sport. So before giving up on sports altogether, people should try a few different non-team sports.

Lesson 5 Writing Action Statements

1. Review the purpose of a persuasive essay. Then say: **Strong persuasive essays have action statements. An action statement should address the issue that the writer describes in the essay and should state specifically what the writer wants the readers to do. Your action statement should be a reasonable, not extreme, response to the problem.**

2. Have students identify the action statement in the writing model on p. 103. *(Encourage the students you know to watch only one hour of TV a day or less.)* Point out that the action statement is usually written in the conclusion. Ask: **Does this sentence address the problem?** (yes) **How is it a reasonable response?** (It addresses the topic and is not too extreme.) **Do you know what the writer wants us to do?** (yes)

3. Direct students to Activity A on p. 107 and discuss the example. Say: **The original action statement does not clearly address the problem.** Then have students complete the activity in small groups. Have students discuss why each action statement needed to be revised. (1. not an appropriate response, 2. does not address the problem, 3. not specific enough)

4. Have students complete Activity B independently. Invite them to share their answers and explain why their sentences are good action statements.

➤ **Extend the Lesson:** Have students write an action statement for the opinion statement they wrote in the Lesson 2 extension activity.

Lesson 6 Reviewing a Persuasive Essay

1. Review the qualities of a good persuasive essay: a strong opinion statement, good reasons and supporting examples, an opposing reason and response, and an action statement.

2. Have students read "Don't Give Up on Sports" on p. 108 and discuss what might be improved. For example, ask: **What are some sports that the writer could list?** (swimming, gymnastics, hiking, dancing, martial arts, etc.) Also, tell students to correct any grammar, punctuation, and spelling errors in the draft.

3. Have students revise the essay independently on a separate sheet of paper. Remind them that there are many ways to fix the essay. Also remind them to proofread their revisions and check for errors. Invite students to share their revisions with the class.

Name: _____

Introducing a Persuasive Essay

Read this example of a persuasive essay.

Writing Model

Turn Off the TV

   Most students spend about four hours a day watching TV. That is too long for anyone to sit still, and it shows. Watching TV harms students' ability to learn and stay healthy, so students should watch less television each day.

   Students who watch a lot of TV often have trouble at school. They usually have lower grades and more behavior problems than students who watch little or no TV. They might even have trouble concentrating in class. Also, students who spend most of their time watching TV have less time to read or do their homework.

   Too much TV time can also be harmful to a student's health. When people watch TV, they are sitting still and not moving. Inactivity leads to poor fitness. In fact, students who watch a lot of TV are more likely to be overweight because they exercise less than other students. And on top of that, students often eat unhealthy snacks such as chips and cookies while watching TV.

   Some people believe that TV is not bad for students as long as they watch educational shows. Although educational shows do teach students, kids should not watch too many of them. No matter what they watch, students are still sitting in front of the TV for long periods of time.

   Encourage the students you know to watch only one hour of TV a day or less. That way, they can keep up their grades, stay healthy, and still enjoy a little TV time.

Writer's Purpose: _____

_____

Name: _____

Writing an Opinion Statement

A. Read each paragraph. Revise the underlined opinion statement so that it is clear and takes a stand.

1.　　School buses are not as safe as people think. Because buses do not have seat belts, students move around a lot. And if there were a wreck, students could even be thrown from their seats. Students who ride school buses need help.

_____

_____

2.　　The world is smaller because of new technologies. People around the world can talk to each other very easily. They can learn a lot from each other. But students in most schools cannot talk to people in other countries because they do not learn a foreign language until high school. Elementary schools in America do not have foreign language classes.

_____

_____

B. Write a strong opinion statement for each topic.

1. **Topic:** keeping animals in zoos

_____

_____

2. **Topic:** selling sodas in school

_____

_____

3. **Topic:** going to school on Saturday

_____

_____

Including Reasons and Examples

A. Fill in the graphic organizer with a reason and three examples that support the opinion statement.

Opinion statement: Teachers should not assign homework on Fridays.

Reason: _____

_____

Example 1: _____

_____

Example 2: _____

_____

Example 3: _____

_____

B. Use the information from the organizer in Activity A to write a persuasive paragraph.

_____

_____

_____

_____

_____

Including an Opposing Reason and a Response

Read each opinion statement. Then write a possible reason against it and a response to that reason.

Example

Lakeland Elementary should switch to energy-saving light bulbs.

Reason against: <u>The switch would cost a lot of money.</u>

Response: <u>The school would save more money over time.</u>

1. Students should have to do volunteer work in their community.

Reason against: _____

Response: _____

_____

2. The computer lab should be open to students for an hour before and after school.

Reason against: _____

Response: _____

3. Students should be required to sell fruit instead of candy to raise money for the school.

Reason against: _____

Response: _____

4. Ashton Elementary should start a food bank for its students and their families.

Reason against: _____

Response: _____

5. The cafeteria should lower the price of lunches.

Reason against: _____

Response: _____

Writing Action Statements

A. Revise each action statement.

> **Example**
>
> **Problem:** The cafeteria never changes its menu.
> **Action statement:** Get the cafeteria to serve ice cream.
>
> **Revised statement:** <u>Ask the cafeteria manager to serve</u>
> <u>a new meal once a week.</u>

1. **Problem:** There are too many plastic bags in landfills.

   Action statement: Never go to a store again.

   Revised statement: _____

   _____

2. **Problem:** Educational video games are not used enough in school.

   Action statement: Play more video games at home.

   Revised statement: _____

   _____

3. **Problem:** The school has canceled all field trips because of lack of money.

   Action statement: Think about what you can do.

   Revised statement: _____

   _____

B. Write an action statement for each problem.

1. **Problem:** The library was flooded, and many books were ruined.

   Action statement: _____

2. **Problem:** The public school does not offer swim lessons.

   Action statement: _____

   _____

Name: _____

Reviewing a Persuasive Essay

Revise this persuasive essay. Think about what you have learned to make it stronger. Rewrite the essay on a separate sheet of paper.

Focus on:

✓ writing a clear opinion statement
✓ including examples that support the reasons
✓ addressing a possible argument and writing a rebuttal
✓ writing an action statement
✓ correcting grammar, punctuation, and spelling errors

Draft

Don't Give Up on Sports

Millions of people play sports. They play soccer, football, basketball, and, baseball. But there are millions of other people out there who do not play sports. because they do not like team sports. However, people should think about maybe trying something else

Sports that do not rekwire playing on a team can help people get the exercise they need.

Sports that do not have teams still bring people together. Kids and adults of all ages participate in them.

Some people disagree with me.

People should never think they cannot be athletes. Most likely. They just have not found the rite sport. People should try every sport there is before giving up on sports altogether.

Writing a Review

Page 112 / Student Book Page 80

Lesson 1 Introducing a Review

A review is a piece of writing that gives important information and expresses an opinion about a book, movie, show, restaurant, or product.

1. Lead a discussion about ways that people learn about new movies, games, books, or restaurants. (word of mouth, ads, etc.) Explain that a review is another way that important information and opinions are shared about things that people are interested in.

2. Have students read the model on p. 112. Then ask: **What is the purpose of this review?** (to give information and the writer's opinion of *Journey to Jupiter*) Have students write the purpose on the lines provided.

3. Invite students to offer opinions about what makes this a good review. Prompt students by asking: **Does the review include important information about the movie? Does the writer state her opinions clearly? Does she give reasons and details from the movie to support her opinion?**

➤ **Extend the Lesson:** Collect reviews from newspapers, magazines, and Web sites for students to discuss.

Lesson 2 Including Important Information

1. Explain that a review should include basic information that the reader would need or want to know about the thing being reviewed. Say: **The type of information that is needed depends on what is being reviewed. For example, what would you need to know about a movie?** (plot, where it is playing, etc.)

2. Direct students to the model movie review on p. 112. Then ask: **Not counting the writer's opinion, what information about the movie is in this review?** (title, what it is about, who is in it, rating, where it is playing, and its length)

3. Direct students to p. 113 and discuss the different kinds of information needed for each type of review. Explain that students might not know all the information that goes in each chart, and that people who write reviews often must do research to find information such as prices, times, etc.

4. Guide students to resources where they can find the information they need. (e.g., shopping Web site to find a price) Have students complete the activity.

Page 112 / Student Book Page 80

Name: _____

Review

Introducing a Review

Read this example of a review.

> **Writing Model**
>
> #### Don't Take This *Journey*
>
> *Journey to Jupiter* begins with a great idea but ends up disappointing viewers with a silly story and bad acting.
>
> The movie is set on a spaceship called the *Journey*. In the movie, Earth's resources had been used up years ago, so people live in colonies on giant ships throughout the solar system. After the captain of the *Journey* mysteriously disappears, it is up to the first mate to get the colony to Jupiter so they can find minerals to power the ship.
>
> After the captain disappears, the movie just becomes silly. Pirates attack the ship, but instead of looking like characters from outer space, they are dressed as old-fashioned pirates with wooden legs and eye patches. And the pirates never explain why they attack.
>
> The acting is almost as bad as the plot. Heather Vale stars as Sully, the first mate who has to save the ship. Her performance is stiff and boring. The pirate captain is played by Ronnie Hepp. All he does is look mean and constantly say "Argh!" Riley Russ plays the first mate's daughter. She gives the only good performance in the movie as the tough and intelligent Mikayla.
>
> *Journey to Jupiter* is a journey better off not taken. Even though it begins with an interesting idea, the bad acting and silly plot take the movie way off course. But if you really want to see a space pirate, *Journey to Jupiter* is playing at Twin Trees Theater and Cinema 25. It is 112 minutes and rated PG.

Writer's Purpose: to give information and the writer's opinion of *Journey to Jupiter*

112   PERSUASIVE WRITING   Nonfiction Writing • EMC 6015 • © Evan-Moor Corp.

Page 113 / Student Book Page 81

Name: _____

Review

Including Important Information

Choose a movie or TV show, a game or toy, and a book you know. Then fill in the charts with basic information you would include in a review for each one.

1. **Movie or TV Show**

Title: Journey to Jupiter	Length: 112 minutes
Starring: Heather Vale, Riley Russ, Ronnie Hepp	What it is about: People live on giant spaceships. Space pirates attack.
Rating: PG	Movie theater or TV channel: Twin Trees Theater and Cinema 25

2. **Game or Toy**

Name: Take Five card game	Cost: $9.99
Company that makes it: True Toys	Parts: 40 cards
Where to buy it: Bull's-eye stores	What is special about it: It is fun and easy to play anywhere.

3. **Book**

Title: The Bad Beginning	Author: Lemony Snicket
What it is about: three orphans adopted by an evil man	Number of pages: 162
Date published: 1999	Publisher: HarperCollins

© Evan-Moor Corp. • EMC 6015 • Nonfiction Writing   PERSUASIVE WRITING 113

Page 114 / Student Book Page 82

Name: _____

Review

Supporting Your Opinion

Name a real example of something in each category that you have an opinion about. Write an opinion statement, and then write a reason and one detail to support your position.

1. A restaurant I have eaten at: Top Taco Shop
   Opinion: Top Taco Shop's food is worth the price.
   Reason: Their tacos are delicious.
   Detail: Tacos come with juicy meat and tangy cheese.

2. A TV show I have watched: Pop Star
   Opinion: Pop Star is the best show on TV.
   Reason: Every week is unpredictable.
   Detail: Each week, the audience votes for the best singer.

3. A toy I have played with: Gross Goop
   Opinion: Gross Goop is not fun to play with.
   Reason: It is very messy!
   Detail: It stains your hands and clothes.

4. A product I have used: Toro Company backpack
   Opinion: Toro Company backpacks are a waste of money.
   Reason: The backpacks are not big enough.
   Detail: They can hold only two books.

5. A movie I have seen: Dainty Dogs in the City
   Opinion: Dainty Dogs in the City is a great movie for kids.
   Reason: The dogs are very silly.
   Detail: One dog always tells bad jokes.

114   PERSUASIVE WRITING   Nonfiction Writing • EMC 6015 • © Evan-Moor Corp.

---

5. Invite pairs to share their completed charts and explain how that information would help them write a review.

➤ **Extend the Lesson:** Reproduce p. 113 again. Have students complete a chart with information from a review they read in the Lesson 1 extension activity.

Lesson 3 Supporting Your Opinion

1. Explain that a review should have sentences that clearly state the writer's opinion about what is being reviewed. Write the following on the board:

   Opinion: Rose's Ride is the best new video game of the year.

   Reason: The graphics make players feel as if they are part of the game.

   Details: The game has bright colors, detailed characters, and exciting backgrounds.

   Explain that the opinion statement clearly states the writer's opinion, the reason tells why the writer believes that the game is the best, and the details support the reason by telling more about the graphics.

2. Have students find the opinion statement in the model movie review on p. 112. (Journey to Jupiter *begins with a great idea but ends up disappointing viewers with a silly story and bad acting.*) Say: **This sentence clearly tells us the writer's opinion about the movie. And the writer doesn't just state that the movie was bad. She gives reasons by telling why the movie was bad.** Then ask: **What details support her claim that the movie was bad?** (e.g., bad costumes, no explanation for why the space pirates attack; bad acting)

3. Have students complete p. 114 independently or in pairs. Invite volunteers to share their answers. Discuss how each reason supports the opinion and how the details support the reason.

➤ **Extend the Lesson:** Have students annotate the reviews from the Lesson 1 extension activity by circling reasons and underlining details.

Lesson 4 Using a Balanced Voice

1. Remind students that "voice" is how their writing sounds when it is read. Say: **The voice of your review should be interesting and opinionated, but it should not be too enthusiastic or too negative. It's important to be fair and thoughtful so people trust your review. It is also important to be specific so your readers understand what you are reviewing.**

2. Have students reread the model on p. 112. Ask: **Is the voice in this review balanced? Why or why not?** (The voice is balanced because it offers an opinion that is positive and negative.) Then have students identify interesting and specific details. Point out that the writer gives clear and interesting details from the movie to make her review more interesting. (e.g., *Pirates attack the ship, but …*)

3. Have students complete the activity on p. 115 in small groups. As needed, guide groups through the example reviews to help them identify how each review could be improved. Invite volunteers to read their revised reviews.

Lesson 5 Reviewing a Written Review

1. Help students recall the qualities of a good review: important basic information, opinions that are supported with reasons and details, and a balanced voice.

2. On the board, write the following additional information about the fictional restaurant in "New Pizza in Town" on p. 116:

Location: 1616 Alvarado Street
Hours: 11 A.M. to 11 P.M.
Most Popular Item: Checkers Supreme Pizza
Cost: $12 to $25 per pizza

3. Have students read the review on p. 116 and discuss what might be improved. For example, ask: **What information about the restaurant is missing from the review?** (where it is, hours, prices) **Is the opinion clearly stated in the beginning?** (no) **What details could you add to the review?** (e.g., choices of toppings, what's good about the Supreme, etc.) Encourage students to include their own ideas or to use details from their favorites places to eat to make this review unique and interesting. Also, tell students to correct any grammar, punctuation, and spelling errors in the draft.

4. Have students rewrite the review independently on a separate sheet of paper. Remind students that there are different ways to improve the review. Also remind them to proofread their revisions and check for errors.

5. Invite volunteers to read aloud their revisions.

Page 115 / Student Book Page 83

Page 116 and Sample Revision / Student Book Page 84

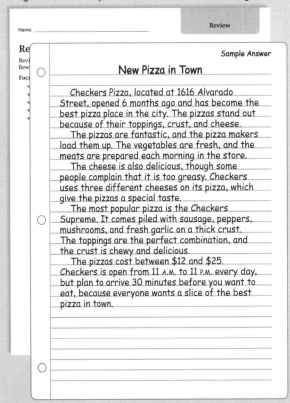

Name: _____

Introducing a Review

Read this example of a review.

Writing Model

Don't Take This *Journey*

Journey to Jupiter begins with a great idea but ends up disappointing viewers with a silly story and bad acting.

The movie is set on a spaceship called the *Journey*. In the movie, Earth's resources had been used up years ago, so people live in colonies on giant ships throughout the solar system. After the captain of the *Journey* mysteriously disappears, it is up to the first mate to get the colony to Jupiter so they can find minerals to power the ship.

After the captain disappears, the movie just becomes silly. Pirates attack the ship, but instead of looking like characters from outer space, they are dressed as old-fashioned pirates with wooden legs and eye patches. And the pirates never explain why they attack.

The acting is almost as bad as the plot. Heather Vale stars as Sully, the first mate who has to save the ship. Her performance is stiff and boring. The pirate captain is played by Ronnie Hepp. All he does is look mean and constantly say "Argh!" Riley Russ plays the first mate's daughter. She gives the only good performance in the movie as the tough and intelligent Mikayla.

Journey to Jupiter is a journey better off not taken. Even though it begins with an interesting idea, the bad acting and silly plot take the movie way off course. But if you really want to see a space pirate, *Journey to Jupiter* is playing at Twin Trees Theater and Cinema 25. It is 112 minutes and rated PG.

Writer's Purpose: _____

_____

Name: _____

Including Important Information

Choose a movie or TV show, a game or toy, and a book you know. Then fill in the charts with basic information you would include in a review for each one.

1. Movie or TV Show

Title:	**Length:**
Starring:	**What it is about:**
Rating:	**Movie theater or TV channel:**

2. Game or Toy

Name:	**Cost:**
Company that makes it:	**Parts:**
Where to buy it:	**What is special about it:**

3. Book

Title:	**Author:**
What it is about:	**Number of pages:**
Date published:	**Publisher:**

Supporting Your Opinion

Name a real example of something in each category that you have an opinion about. Write an opinion statement, and then write a reason and one detail to support your position.

1. **A restaurant I have eaten at:** _____

   Opinion: _____

   Reason: _____

   Detail: _____

2. **A TV show I have watched:** _____

   Opinion: _____

   Reason: _____

   Detail: _____

3. **A toy I have played with:** _____

   Opinion: _____

   Reason: _____

   Detail: _____

4. **A product I have used:** _____

   Opinion: _____

   Reason: _____

   Detail: _____

5. **A movie I have seen:** _____

   Opinion: _____

   Reason: _____

   Detail: _____

Using a Balanced Voice

1. The following review is too positive and nonspecific to be trustworthy. Revise it to give it a more balanced voice.

   Rainbow Pencils are the best colored pencils ever made! You will not find nicer colors anywhere. They break often, which means you get a lot of exercise walking to and from the sharpener. But you can draw thin and thick lines with them.

   _____

   _____

   _____

   _____

2. This review is too negative to be trustworthy. Revise it to have a more balanced voice.

   The game Race Trax is the most boring game ever invented. The object of this pointless game is to move a race car five laps around the board. And the rules are so complicated that only geniuses can play, if they have a million hours to waste! Anyone who plays this horrible game will fall asleep before it's over.

   _____

   _____

   _____

   _____

3. This review is too vague and uninteresting. Revise it to have a more interesting voice.

   The box for Toasty Oaties looks bad. The cereal tastes good. The flavors are nice. There's fruit and stuff in the cereal. The nutrition is good.

   _____

   _____

   _____

   _____

Reviewing a Written Review

Revise this review. Use what you have learned to make it stronger.
Rewrite the review on a separate sheet of paper.

Focus on:

✓ including important basic information about the restaurant
✓ writing a clear opinion statement
✓ including reasons and details that support the opinion statement
✓ using an interesting and balanced voice
✓ correcting grammar, punctuation, and spelling errors

Draft

New Pizza in Town

Checkers Pizza only opened about 6 months ago, but there are already lines of people waiting to get in.

The toppings on the pizza's are the most amazing ever, and the pizza makers pile them on. There are vegtables and meats.

The cheese is good, some people think it is too greasy. Checkers uses three diferent cheeses on it's pizzas, which gives the pizzas a special taste. The most popular pizza is the Checkers Supreme.

Checkers is open every day, plan to arrive 30 minutes before you want to eat because everyone wants a slice of the best pizza in town.

Writing an Editorial

Lesson 1 Introducing an Editorial

An editorial is a piece of writing that appears in a newspaper or magazine and expresses the writer's opinions and ideas about a current event or issue.

1. Explain that most editorials are about current news events or issues that affect a community. Say: **The writer is trying to persuade the audience to agree with his or her position on the event or issue.** Explain that most editorials are found in newspapers or magazines and that newspapers place editorials together in a special section. Ask: **Why do you think that is?** (so that readers know they are reading opinions, rather than news stories)

2. Have students read the model on p. 120. Then ask: **What is the purpose of this editorial?** (to persuade people in Shelbyville to foster a pet) Have students write the purpose on the lines provided.

3. Invite students to offer opinions about what makes this a good editorial. Prompt students by asking: **Does the writer clearly identify and explain a single issue? Does she give her opinion about the issue? Does she answer an argument against her opinion? Does she clearly tell readers what to do about the issue?**

➤ **Extend the Lesson:** Have students read other editorials from newspapers and magazines. Ask them to identify the topic and purpose of each editorial.

Lesson 2 Writing an Introduction

1. Review the purpose of an editorial. Then say: **The introduction to an editorial does two things. First, it introduces the topic or issue and gives important background information for the reader. Second, the introduction gives the writer's position on the topic or issue.**

2. Direct students to the model on p. 120 and ask: **What is the topic of this editorial?** (fostering a pet) **What background information does the writer give about the topic in the introduction?** (She tells more about the animals that are in shelters.) Then have students find the sentence that explains the writer's position. *(People who are considering ...)* Say: **This paragraph introduces the topic, gives important information about animals in shelters for people who may not be familiar with them, and states the writer's position.**

Page 120 / Student Book Page 86

Name: _____

Editorial

Introducing an Editorial
Read this example of an editorial.

Writing Model

Foster a Shelbyville Pet

Most people in Shelbyville who want a new pet want one that is young, cute, healthy, and sweet. But not every animal in our town's shelter is like that. Some animals are older, and some have health problems. A few animals are scared of people because they came to the shelter from homes where they were harmed or neglected. But these animals need care, and many people in Shelbyville would benefit from having a foster animal. People who are considering adopting a pet should foster one first.

Fostering an animal means that a person brings an animal home and cares for it for a few days or even a few months. By fostering a pet, new pet owners can learn what types of animals they like best. They also see how much time and effort it takes to care for a pet. This will help better prepare them for a permanent pet of their own.

Fostering a pet is good for the animals, too. Animals get better care at a foster home than they do in a shelter. The animals also get a second chance to live in a home. Animals that are scared of people or that have problems behaving can learn how to be better pets in a foster home.

Some people might think that fostering animals for a short time is a bad idea because it is hard on the animals when they are later separated from their foster owners. But most animals that go to foster homes have a better chance of being adopted into permanent homes. In fact, most of the animals that are fostered are often happier and better behaved after the experience.

Animals deserve to have the best permanent home possible, but those homes can be hard to find. In the meantime, people who are thinking about adopting a pet should go to the Shelbyville Animal Rescue and foster an animal.

Writer's Purpose: to persuade people in Shelbyville to foster a pet

120 **PERSUASIVE WRITING**   Nonfiction Writing • EMC 6015 • © Evan-Moor Corp.

Writing an Editorial, continued

Page 121 / Student Book Page 87

Name: _____

Editorial

Writing an Introduction

A. Read the introduction below. Underline the sentences that give background information that help you better understand the topic. Double-underline the sentence that states the writer's position.

Last month, the mural at Johnson Middle School was vandalized by graffiti. The mural, which was painted in 2002 and showed a large group of kids playing together, is the first thing that school visitors see. But someone ruined the mural by spraying black paint across it. Teachers and parents want to repaint the damaged parts of the mural, but the principal claims that the school does not have money in the budget to do so. This is why the community should donate the materials and time needed to repair the mural.

B. Read the topic and the background information about video game ratings. Then write an introduction for an editorial about whether kids should be able to buy video games without restrictions. Be sure your introduction gives important information and states your opinion.

In 2010, $18 billion worth of video games were sold. Only 5 percent of games in 2010 have a "mature" rating. This is a rating given to video games with extreme violence. Most stores will not sell games with this rating to children without a parent's permission. However, over 50 percent of gamers between the ages of 12 and 17 have at least one game with a "mature" rating that was bought by a parent or relative. It is illegal to ban the sale of video games to kids, but many teachers and parents want some kind of ban.

Stores have policies against selling games with a "mature" rating to kids. However, more than half of all gamers own at least one violent video game that was bought for them by a parent or relative. Banning the sale of video games to kids is illegal. This is why kids should be allowed to buy any video game, including violent ones.

© Evan-Moor Corp. • EMC 6015 • Nonfiction Writing ⠀⠀⠀⠀ PERSUASIVE WRITING 121

Page 122 / Student Book Page 88

Name: _____

Editorial

Responding to Other People's Arguments

A. Read each opinion. Then write an argument against that opinion.

> **Example**
> **Opinion:** The sidewalks near schools should be repaired because there are many places where the concrete is broken.
> **Argument:** The city should not spend money on repairing sidewalks when it has other budget problems that are more important.

1. **Opinion:** The mall should have more bike racks.
   Argument: Few people ride their bikes to the mall.

2. **Opinion:** People should eat less food and more home-cooked meals.
   Argument: Some people do not have time to cook.

B. Read each opinion and the argument against it. Then write a response to that argument.

1. **Opinion:** Kids look up to celebrities too much.
   Argument: Many celebrities deserve to be looked up to because they give to charity.
   Response: There are people whom kids can meet in their own towns who do good deeds.

2. **Opinion:** Teachers do not use enough technology in their classrooms.
   Argument: Teachers may not know how to use some forms of technology.
   Response: Teachers need to learn how to use technology so they can make school more interesting for students.

122 PERSUASIVE WRITING ⠀⠀⠀ Nonfiction Writing • EMC 6015 • © Evan-Moor Corp.

---

3. Direct students' attention to Activity A on p. 121. Read aloud the directions and then have a volunteer read aloud the introduction. Guide students through the activity and discuss whether or not each sentence gives background information about the topic (e.g., the second and third sentences) or the problem (e.g., the third sentence) and how important or helpful the information is.

4. For Activity B, read aloud the directions and then have students read the background information. Briefly discuss the topic to make sure that students understand the content. Then have students complete the activity.

➤ **Extend the Lesson:** Challenge students to complete Activity B again, this time taking the opposite position. Encourage them to think about how the background information they use in the new introduction differs from the information they used previously.

Lesson 3 Responding to Other People's Arguments

1. Review the purpose of an editorial. Then say: **In order to persuade your readers, sometimes you need to respond to people who disagree with your position. You should acknowledge the argument against your position and then explain why you think that argument is wrong or why your opinion is better.**

2. Direct students' attention to the model on p. 120 and read aloud paragraph 4. Then ask: **What possible argument against fostering animals does the writer acknowledge?** (separating an animal from its foster home might harm it) **What is her response?** (Foster animals are likely to later find a permanent home.)

3. Direct students to p. 122. Read aloud the directions for Activity A and discuss the example with students. Then have students complete the activity in small groups. Remind students that there is more than one possible argument for each opinion.

4. Have students complete Activity B. If necessary, complete the first item as a class.

➤ **Extend the Lesson:** Have students read newspaper and magazine editorials to find opposing arguments and responses. Discuss with students if addressing those arguments made the editorials more persuasive.

Lesson 4 Writing a Call to Action

1. Review the purpose of an editorial. Then say: **An editorial should have a statement that tells your readers what you want them to do about the issue you are writing about. This is the "call to action."**

2. Direct students to the model on p. 120 and have a volunteer read aloud the last paragraph. Ask: **Which sentence gives the call to action?** *(In the meantime, …)* **Is this call to action clear and specific?** (yes) **Does it support the writer's position?** (yes)

3. Direct students to the activity on p. 123 and have a volunteer read aloud the example. Then invite students to suggest other possible calls to action. Ask: **How else could people help hurricane victims?** (help clean up, provide temporary places for people to stay, etc.) Have students complete the activity in pairs, and encourage partners to discuss various calls to action for each opinion before picking the best one. Invite volunteers to share their responses.

➤ **Extend the Lesson:** Have groups of students brainstorm issues affecting their community. Then have them write a call to action for each issue and discuss how to make each call to action clearer and more specific.

Lesson 5 Reviewing an Editorial

1. Review the qualities of a good editorial: an introduction that introduces the topic and states the writer's opinion, an opposing argument and response, and a call to action.

2. Have students read "Do Something at School" on p. 124 and discuss what might be improved. For example, help students determine the issue the writer wants to discuss (having a day for games at school). Then ask: **Does the introduction state the issue clearly?** (no) Also, tell students to correct any grammar, punctuation, and spelling errors in the draft.

3. Have students rewrite the editorial independently on a separate sheet of paper. Remind them that there may be different ways to improve the editorial. Also remind them to proofread their revisions and check for errors.

4. Invite students to share their revisions with the class.

Page 123 / Student Book Page 89

Name: _____

Editorial

Writing a Call to Action

Read each opinion and then write a call to action.

Example

Opinion: Many people in the community had their lives ruined by the hurricane.
Call to action: Help hurricane victims by donating money and supplies.

1. Healthy snacks, such as yogurt or carrots, are good for children.
Let your kids eat healthy snacks.

2. The Main Street library does not have enough graphic novels.
Ask the librarians to purchase more graphic novels.

3. The broken swing set on the playground is dangerous.
Replace the playground swing set with something safer.

4. School should start a week later so that students can attend the state fair.
Call the school office and ask that school start later.

5. The community pool is unsafe because many people do not follow the rules.
Report dangerous behavior to the lifeguards.

6. The school's cleaning supplies are full of dangerous chemicals.
Ask the school to use safer cleaning supplies.

7. Adults do not understand the pressure students feel when they take a test.
Bring home a test for your parents to try taking.

8. The water from the park's drinking fountains is gross and smells like rotten eggs.
Write a letter asking the city to fix the fountains.

© Evan-Moor Corp. • EMC 6015 • Nonfiction Writing   PERSUASIVE WRITING   123

Page 124 and Sample Revision / Student Book Page 90

Name: _____

Editorial

Sample Answer

Game Day at School

School is tough for students. Every day seems filled with tests or practicing for tests. Students, teachers, and principals are all stressed out. We need a day when everyone in the school just plays games.

Playing games has many benefits. Games such as football and baseball are good exercise. They also give kids the chance to work together on a team. Video games are relaxing and help kids learn to solve problems. And games such as tag and hide-and-seek are a lot of fun to play.

Playing games at school will help students and teachers have less stress. It will also give students a break from all the work they have to do. And having fun in school means more kids will like school.

Some people might say that school is meant only for learning, but this is not true. Learning is important, but having time to play and rest your brain is important, too.

Having a game day is important for students. If you think a day for games is important, too, please go to the school board meeting on Wednesday and tell them how you feel.

Introducing an Editorial

Read this example of an editorial.

Writing Model

Foster a Shelbyville Pet

Most people in Shelbyville who want a new pet want one that is young, cute, healthy, and sweet. But not every animal in our town's shelter is like that. Some animals are older, and some have health problems. A few animals are scared of people because they came to the shelter from homes where they were harmed or neglected. But these animals need care, and many people in Shelbyville would benefit from having a foster animal. People who are considering adopting a pet should foster one first.

Fostering an animal means that a person brings an animal home and cares for it for a few days or even a few months. By fostering a pet, new pet owners can learn what types of animals they like best. They also see how much time and effort it takes to care for a pet. This will help better prepare them for a permanent pet of their own.

Fostering a pet is good for the animals, too. Animals get better care at a foster home than they do in a shelter. The animals also get a second chance to live in a home. Animals that are scared of people or that have problems behaving can learn how to be better pets in a foster home.

Some people might think that fostering animals for a short time is a bad idea because it is hard on the animals when they are later separated from their foster owners. But most animals that go to foster homes have a better chance of being adopted into permanent homes. In fact, most of the animals that are fostered are often happier and better behaved after the experience.

Animals deserve to have the best permanent home possible, but those homes can be hard to find. In the meantime, people who are thinking about adopting a pet should go to the Shelbyville Animal Rescue and foster an animal.

Writer's Purpose: _____

_____

Writing an Introduction

A. Read the introduction below. Underline the sentences that give background information that help you better understand the topic. Double-underline the sentence that states the writer's position.

Last month, the mural at Johnson Middle School was vandalized by graffiti. The mural, which was painted in 2002 and showed a large group of kids playing together, is the first thing that school visitors see. But someone ruined the mural by spraying black paint across it. Teachers and parents want to repaint the damaged parts of the mural, but the principal claims that the school does not have money in the budget to do so. This is why the community should donate the materials and time needed to repair the mural.

B. Read the topic and the background information about video game ratings. Then write an introduction for an editorial about whether kids should be able to buy video games without restrictions. Be sure your introduction gives important information and states your opinion.

In 2010, $18 billion worth of video games were sold. Only 5 percent of games in 2010 have a "mature" rating. This is a rating given to video games with extreme violence. Most stores will not sell games with this rating to children without a parent's permission. However, over 50 percent of gamers between the ages of 12 and 17 have at least one game with a "mature" rating that was bought by a parent or relative. It is illegal to ban the sale of video games to kids, but many teachers and parents want some kind of ban.

_____

_____

_____

_____

_____

_____

Responding to Other People's Arguments

A. Read each opinion. Then write an argument against that opinion.

> **Example**
>
> **Opinion:** The sidewalks near schools should be repaired because there are many places where the concrete is broken.
>
> **Argument:** <u>The city should not spend money on repairing sidewalks when it has other budget problems that are more important.</u>

1. **Opinion:** The mall should have more bike racks.

   Argument: _____

   _____

2. **Opinion:** People should eat less food and more home-cooked meals.

   Argument: _____

   _____

B. Read each opinion and the argument against it. Then write a response to that argument.

1. **Opinion:** Kids look up to celebrities too much.

   Argument: Many celebrities deserve to be looked up to because they give to charity.

   Response: _____

   _____

2. **Opinion:** Teachers do not use enough technology in their classrooms.

   Argument: Teachers may not know how to use some forms of technology.

   Response: _____

   _____

Writing a Call to Action

Read each opinion and then write a call to action.

> **Example**
>
> **Opinion:** Many people in the community had their lives ruined by the hurricane.
> **Call to action:** <u>Help hurricane victims by donating money and supplies.</u>

1. Healthy snacks, such as yogurt or carrots, are good for children.

_____

2. The Main Street library does not have enough graphic novels.

_____

3. The broken swing set on the playground is dangerous.

_____

4. School should start a week later so that students can attend the state fair.

_____

5. The community pool is unsafe because many people do not follow the rules.

_____

6. The school's cleaning supplies are full of dangerous chemicals.

_____

7. Adults do not understand the pressure students feel when they take a test.

_____

8. The water from the park's drinking fountains is gross and smells like rotten eggs.

_____

Reviewing an Editorial

Revise this editorial. Use what you have learned to make it stronger.
Rewrite it on a separate sheet of paper.

Focus on:

✓ writing a clear sentence that states the issue and opinion
✓ considering a possible argument against the opinion and giving a response to that argument
✓ writing a clear and specific call to action
✓ correcting grammar, punctuation, and spelling errors

Draft

Game Day at School

School is tough for students. Every minute of the day, seams filled with tests or practicing for tests. Students, teachers, and principles are all stressed out. A day should be set aside.

Playing games have many benefits. Some games are football and baseball. They also give kids the chance to work together on a team. Video games is relaxing and help kids learn to solve problems.

Playing games at school will helps students and teachers have less stress. It also gives students a brake from all the work they have to do. And having fun in school means more students will like school.

Some people might say that school is meant only for learning, but this is not true. Games such as hide-and-seek and tag are a lot of fun to play.

Having a day for games is important four students.

Writing a Problem-Solution Essay

Lesson 1   Introducing a Problem-Solution Essay

A problem-solution essay explains a specific, concrete problem and proposes a possible solution for it.

1. Say: **When you want to explain a problem and then propose a possible solution for that problem, you should write a problem-solution essay. A problem-solution essay is a good way to persuade people to solve a specific problem.**

2. Have volunteers read aloud the model on p. 128. Ask: **What is the problem mentioned in the essay?** (eating without thinking) **What is the writer's solution?** (keeping a food journal) Have students write the problem and solution on the lines provided.

3. Invite students to offer opinions about what makes this a good problem-solution essay. Prompt by asking: **Does the writer clearly state the problem? Does the writer explain why the problem should be solved? Does the writer clearly state a solution? Is the solution supported with good reasons and details? Is the essay organized in a way that makes it easy to understand?**

Lesson 2   Stating the Problem

1. Remind students of the purpose of a problem-solution essay. Then say: **Good problem-solution essays discuss problems that have reasonable solutions. What are some problems that would be extremely difficult or impossible to solve?** (e.g., war, world hunger) **The problem should not be a personal complaint, either, such as having a bratty sister. And the problem should be clearly stated so the reader can easily understand it.** Ask students to identify the topic sentence that states the problem in the model on p. 128. (*This kind of mindless eating is a problem because it can lead to poor health.*) Ask: **Why is this a good statement of the problem?** (It is clearly stated, it is solvable, and it is not a personal complaint.)

2. Direct students to Activity A on p. 129 and read the directions aloud. Guide them through the first item. Ask: **Which sentence is a personal complaint?** (the first) **Which sentence does not state a problem or is unclear about what problem the writer wants to solve?** (the third) **Which sentence would be the best topic sentence for a problem-solution essay?** (the second) Have students complete the activity independently. Review the answers as a class.

Page 128 / Student Book Page 92

Name: _____

Problem-Solution Essay

Introducing a Problem-Solution Essay

Read this example of a problem-solution essay.

Writing Model

Write What You Eat

A lot of people do not think about what they eat. They just eat when they are hungry and do not pay much attention to their food. In fact, many people probably cannot even remember everything that they ate yesterday! This kind of mindless eating is a problem because it can lead to poor health.

When people do not think about the food they eat, they can eat too much or make poor food choices. For instance, it is easy to gobble up an entire bag of chips while watching TV or to eat a giant box of candy while sitting at the movies. Or when a person is in a rush and does not focus on what to eat, he or she might choose an unhealthy meal that is high in calories and low in nutrition.

A good solution to this problem is for people to keep a food journal. People are less likely to eat large amounts of food when they have to write down what they are eating. Plus, keeping a food journal helps people notice the kinds of food choices they are making. This awareness makes them more likely to choose meals that are low in calories and high in nutrition.

Keeping a food journal does not require a lot of time. It only takes a few minutes after each meal or snack. It's not necessary to keep a food journal forever. Writing a journal for just one week or one month can be enough time for most people to learn about the foods they eat. Then they can start forming truly healthy eating habits.

Problem: eating without thinking about the food

Solution: keeping a food journal

128   PERSUASIVE WRITING   Nonfiction Writing • EMC 6015 • © Evan-Moor Corp.

Page 129 / Student Book Page 93

Name: _____

Problem-Solution Essay

Stating the Problem

A. Read each set of sentences. Underline the sentence that would be the best topic sentence for a problem-solution essay. Look for the sentence that clearly states a solvable problem that is not a personal complaint.

1. I don't know anything about my neighbors.
   <u>Some neighbors do not know each other well enough.</u>
   All neighbors are strangers.

2. <u>Bike riders do not always know how to safely ride their bikes in traffic.</u>
   My sister does not like the bike helmet she bought.
   Every street, road, and highway in the city needs a bike lane.

3. My mom talks during movies.
   <u>People who talk during movies bother those around them.</u>
   Making any kind of noise in a theater ruins the movie for everyone else.

B. Each problem below is either a personal gripe, is too big to solve, or is not clearly stated. Revise each statement to make it stronger.

1. It took me twenty minutes to open the new game because there was so much plastic around it.
   <u>Games often come wrapped in too much plastic packaging.</u>

2. Sometimes students have to miss school.
   <u>When students miss school, they often fall behind.</u>

3. I can never find an empty chair when I want to sit beside the pool.
   <u>The pool does not have enough chairs so people can relax.</u>

4. Something has to be done about homeless animals.
   <u>Too many people buy pets at stores instead of adopting them at shelters.</u>

© Evan-Moor Corp. • EMC 6015 • Nonfiction Writing   PERSUASIVE WRITING   129

Writing a Problem-Solution Essay, continued

Page 130 / Student Book Page 94

Name: _____

Problem-Solution Essay

Supporting the Solution

A. Read each paragraph. Then write a reason or a detail that explains more about the solution.

1. Students do not have time after school to finish all of their homework. To solve this problem, teachers should assign only 30 minutes of homework a night.

   <u>Most students have time to complete 30 minutes</u>
   <u>of homework.</u>

2. There are too many old books in the library that students do not want to read. One solution for this is to allow students to choose new books for the library.

   <u>Students will choose popular books that other students</u>
   <u>will want to read.</u>

3. Dogs can get hurt if they are tied up outside and left alone for a long time. The city should pass a law against leaving dogs tied up for more than an hour.

   <u>People will think more carefully about how long they</u>
   <u>plan to be gone before leaving their dogs.</u>

B. Write a solution for each problem. Then write a reason or detail that explains how the solution will solve that problem.

1. **Problem:** The local food bank is running out of food.
   Solution: <u>Restaurants should donate food to the food bank.</u>
   Detail: <u>The food bank won't need to depend only on</u>
   <u>citizens to donate food.</u>

2. **Problem:** School buses give off gases that pollute the environment.
   Solution: <u>Schools should buy electric school buses.</u>
   Detail: <u>Electric buses do not give off toxic gases.</u>

130 **PERSUASIVE WRITING**   Nonfiction Writing • EMC 6015 • © Evan-Moor Corp.

---

3. For Activity B, pair students and point out that there may be multiple ways to revise the statements. Have students trade revised statements with their partner and focus on making their statements clearer. Invite volunteers to share their statements, and discuss as a group if each one would be a good topic sentence for a problem-solution essay.

➤ **Extend the Lesson:** Have students brainstorm problems and then decide if each one fits the criteria for a problem-solution essay. Then have them write a topic sentence for an essay about one of the problems.

Lesson 3 Supporting the Solution

1. Review the purpose of a problem-solution essay. Then say: **The solution to a problem must be supported with good reasons and details that explain how the solution would solve that problem.**

2. Have students identify the solution in "Write What You Eat" on p. 128. (keeping a food journal) Say: **The solution is reasonable, but it is not persuasive by itself. In order to convince readers to keep a food journal, the writer must tell them why it is important by using good reasons and details. What details does the writer give to support the solution?** (People will be aware of what goes into their bodies, will make healthy food choices, etc.)

3. Read aloud the directions on p. 130 and guide students through the first paragraph in Activity A. Ask: **What is the problem?** (Students don't have time to finish homework.) **What is the solution?** (Teachers should assign only 30 minutes of homework.) **What is a detail that would support this solution?** (e.g., Most students have time to complete 30 minutes of homework.) Explain that there can be many supporting details for each solution. Then have students complete the activity in pairs. Review the answers as a class.

4. Have students complete Activity B in pairs. Invite students to share and explain their answers.

➤ **Extend the Lesson:** Have small groups of students write a sentence that introduces a problem and a sentence that gives the solution. Then have them exchange sentences with other groups. Have groups list details that would support the solution they were given.

Lesson 4 Balancing Information

1. Say: **A problem-solution essay should have balanced information. This means that the information that describes the problem and the information that describes the solution should be equally well developed. The details in each paragraph should also come in the same order so that your reader can easily follow along as you describe the problem and solution.**

2. Direct students to the second paragraph of "Write What You Eat" on p. 128. Say: **This paragraph gives details about why eating without thinking is a real problem. Let's number the details in the paragraph.** (1. People eat too much, such as when they are sitting and watching television. 2. People make poor choices, such as when they are in a rush.) Then have students number the details in the solution paragraph. (1. People eat less. 2. People make better choices.)

3. Have students complete the activity on p. 131 in pairs. Invite students to share their revisions with the class.

Lesson 5 Reviewing a Problem-Solution Essay

1. Review the qualities of a good problem-solution essay: a clear, solvable problem; a strong solution; reasons and details that support the solution; and balanced organization.

2. Have students read the essay on p. 132 and discuss what might be improved. For example, make sure they recognize that they need to add details to support the solution. Also, tell students to correct any grammar, punctuation, and spelling errors in the draft.

3. Have students revise the essay independently or in pairs on a separate sheet of paper. Remind them that there are different ways to fix the essay. Also remind them to proofread their revisions and check for errors.

4. Invite students to share their revisions with the class.

Page 131 / Student Book Page 95

Name: _____   Problem-Solution Essay

Balancing Information

Read each set of paragraphs. Revise the second paragraph so that its information is balanced against the first paragraph. You may need to reorganize the order of the sentences or add details to the second paragraph.

1. The Otters will not win any games this season. Their pitcher cannot see well and always throws wild pitches. The players all have holes in their gloves. And all their bats are either dented or broken.
    The team must buy new gloves. The team should get some new bats, too. If the Otters buy new equipment, they might win some games. The pitcher needs to get some glasses, as well.

    If the Otters make sure the players have what they need, they might win some games. The Otters' pitcher should get new glasses. Everyone should get new gloves, and the team should also buy some new bats.

2. The new hamburger restaurant in town has many problems with cleanliness. There are flies everywhere, and the trays they serve food on are always dirty. The trays should be cleaned before customers use them.

    The employees need to clean up the restaurant. Employees need to keep windows and doors closed to keep flies out. The trays should be clean when customers use them.

3. Many students play soccer and baseball, but not enough play tennis or basketball. Few students know there is a tennis team at school. Nobody plays basketball because the pavement on the outdoor basketball court is uneven, and the backboards and hoops are rusted and crooked. The school should do more to interest students in other sports.

    The school should do more to interest students in other sports. The tennis coach should visit each classroom to tell students about the team. The school should fix the basketball court and equipment.

© Evan-Moor Corp. • EMC 6015 • Nonfiction Writing   PERSUASIVE WRITING 131

Page 132 and Sample Revision / Student Book Page 96

Name: _____   Problem-Solution Essay

Sample Answer

What Happened to Leaving Kids Alone?

Many kids spend their time going to school, practicing sports, and taking music lessons. Plus, many kids have homework and chores every night. Kids no longer have time to relax by themselves.

Not having free time is a problem. Kids can become stressed and have trouble concentrating. They have so many planned activities that they do not use their imagination or creativity. Plus, kids miss out on learning how to manage their own time and directing themselves.

The solution to this problem is to limit kids' planned time to two activities a week during their free time. That way, kids will have more time to relax or play. They will have less stress. They will be able to concentrate better at school. Plus, with more free time, kids will use their imagination and creativity to come up with fun things to do. They will also learn how to manage their time and take care of themselves.

Kids need more time to relax. Limiting the number of planned activities in their lives will give them the time they need.

Name: _____

Introducing a Problem-Solution Essay

Read this example of a problem-solution essay.

Writing Model

Write What You Eat

A lot of people do not think about what they eat. They just eat when they are hungry and do not pay much attention to their food. In fact, many people probably cannot even remember everything that they ate yesterday! This kind of mindless eating is a problem because it can lead to poor health.

When people do not think about the food they eat, they can eat too much or make poor food choices. For instance, it is easy to gobble up an entire bag of chips while watching TV or to eat a giant box of candy while sitting at the movies. Or when a person is in a rush and does not focus on what to eat, he or she might choose an unhealthy meal that is high in calories and low in nutrition.

A good solution to this problem is for people to keep a food journal. People are less likely to eat large amounts of food when they have to write down what they are eating. Plus, keeping a food journal helps people notice the kinds of food choices they are making. This awareness makes them more likely to choose meals that are low in calories and high in nutrition.

Keeping a food journal does not require a lot of time. It only takes a few minutes after each meal or snack. It's not necessary to keep a food journal forever. Writing a journal for just one week or one month can be enough time for most people to learn about the foods they eat. Then they can start forming truly healthy eating habits.

Problem: _____

Solution: _____

Name: _____

Stating the Problem

A. Read each set of sentences. Underline the sentence that would be the best topic sentence for a problem-solution essay. Look for the sentence that clearly states a solvable problem that is not a personal complaint.

1. I don't know anything about my neighbors.

   Some neighbors do not know each other well enough.

   All neighbors are strangers.

2. Bike riders do not always know how to safely ride their bikes in traffic.

   My sister does not like the bike helmet she bought.

   Every street, road, and highway in the city needs a bike lane.

3. My mom talks during movies.

   People who talk during movies bother those around them.

   Making any kind of noise in a theater ruins the movie for everyone else.

B. Each problem below is either a personal gripe, is too big to solve, or is not clearly stated. Revise each statement to make it stronger.

1. It took me twenty minutes to open the new game because there was so much plastic around it.

   _____

2. Sometimes students have to miss school.

   _____

3. I can never find an empty chair when I want to sit beside the pool.

   _____

4. Something has to be done about homeless animals.

   _____

   _____

Supporting the Solution

A. Read each paragraph. Then write a reason or a detail that explains more about the solution.

1. Students do not have time after school to finish all of their homework. To solve this problem, teachers should assign only 30 minutes of homework a night.

    _____

    _____

2. There are too many old books in the library that students do not want to read. One solution for this is to allow students to choose new books for the library.

    _____

    _____

3. Dogs can get hurt if they are tied up outside and left alone for a long time. The city should pass a law against leaving dogs tied up for more than an hour.

    _____

    _____

B. Write a solution for each problem. Then write a reason or detail that explains how the solution will solve that problem.

1. **Problem:** The local food bank is running out of food.

    Solution: _____

    Detail: _____

    _____

2. **Problem:** School buses give off gases that pollute the environment.

    Solution: _____

    Detail: _____

    _____

Balancing Information

Read each set of paragraphs. Revise the second paragraph so that its information is balanced against the first paragraph. You may need to reorganize the order of the sentences or add details to the second paragraph.

1.　 The Otters will not win any games this season. Their pitcher cannot see well and always throws wild pitches. The players all have holes in their gloves. And all their bats are either dented or broken.

　　 The team must buy new gloves. The team should get some new bats, too. If the Otters buy new equipment, they might win some games. The pitcher needs to get some glasses, as well.

_____

_____

_____

_____

2.　 The new hamburger restaurant in town has many problems with cleanliness. There are flies everywhere, and the trays they serve food on are always dirty.

　　 The trays should be cleaned before customers use them.

_____

_____

_____

_____

3.　 Many students play soccer and baseball, but not enough play tennis or basketball. Few students know there is a tennis team at school. Nobody plays basketball because the pavement on the outdoor basketball court is uneven, and the backboards and hoops are rusted and crooked.

　　 The school should do more to interest students in other sports.

_____

_____

_____

_____

Name: _____

Reviewing a Problem-Solution Essay

Revise this essay. Use what you have learned to make it stronger.
Rewrite it on a separate sheet of paper.

Focus on:

✓ writing a problem statement that is clear, solvable, and not a personal gripe
✓ supporting the solution with reasons
✓ balancing the information for the problem and solution
✓ correcting grammar, punctuation, and spelling errors

Draft

What Happened to Leaving Kids Alone?

Many kids spend their time going to school, practicing sports, and to take music lessons. Plus, many have homework and chores every night. I'm sick of never having time to just play anymore.

Kids can become stressed out and have trouble consentrating. They have so many planned activities that they do not use their imagination or creativitee. Not halfing free time is a problem. Plus, kids miss out on learning how to solve problems and to manaje their own time.

The solution to this problem, is to limit kids' planned aktivities during their free time to two aktivities each week. Will kids have more time to do whatever they want? Yes.

Kids need more free time in their lives. Limiting the number of planned activities in their lives will give them the free time they need.

Writing a Pro-Con Essay

Lesson 1 Introducing a Pro-Con Essay

A pro-con essay is persuasive writing that gives the arguments for and against an idea or issue and explains why one side of the argument is stronger than the other.

1. Explain that *pro* means *for* and *con* means *against*. Then say: **In a pro-con essay, you should give reasons for and against an idea or issue and tell which side you believe is stronger.**

2. Have students read the model essay on p. 137. Then ask: **What is the purpose of this essay?** (to explain the arguments for and against playing video games and to persuade the reader that there are benefits to playing video games) Have students write the purpose on the lines provided.

3. Invite students to offer opinions about what makes this a good pro-con essay. Prompt students by asking: **Does the introduction catch your attention? Does the writer clearly state what the essay is about? Does the writer explain both sides of the argument? Does he support his opinion with details?**

➤ **Extend the Lesson:** Have students brainstorm topics for a pro-con essay. Suggest that they list topics that have been debated in the school, community, state, or country.

Lesson 2 Establishing Pros and Cons

1. Review the purpose of a pro-con essay. Then say: **It's important to choose a topic that you can make both pro and con statements about. Those statements should be clear and easy to understand. They will become the sentences that express the main idea of your body paragraphs.**

2. On the board, write *pro statement* and *con statement*. Then direct students to paragraphs 2 and 3 in "Is Gaming a Waste of Time?" Ask: **What is the main idea in paragraph 2?** (*Many people worry …*) Write it under *con statement*. Ask: **What is the main idea in paragraph 3?** (*Despite the concerns, children …*) Write it under *pro statement*.

3. Turn students' attention to the activity on p. 138 and read aloud the instructions. Allow small groups of students to discuss the issues before having students complete the activity independently.

Page 137 / Student Book Page 98

Name: _____

Pro-Con Essay

Introducing a Pro-Con Essay

Read this example of a good pro-con essay.

Writing Model

Is Gaming a Waste of Time?

Boys in elementary school spend an average of 13 hours every week playing video games. Girls spend an average of 5 hours gaming each week. Are they wasting their time? While some people think that video games are bad for children, the truth is that gamers learn valuable skills.

Many people worry about the harmful effects of playing video games. For example, some games have a lot of violence in them. And, unfortunately, some children do act more aggressive when they play violent video games. Also, children who spend too much time playing games often do worse in school than kids who do not spend as much time playing. And some adults worry that children who play video games do not get enough exercise.

Despite the concerns, children learn many positive skills when they play video games. Many games require players to solve problems, so players learn critical-thinking skills. And playing a game over and over teaches players to keep trying until they reach their goals. Playing video games also helps players improve their hand-eye coordination, which leads to a stronger brain. Finally, many new and popular video games require children to move around and exercise.

While not everyone supports video games, most parents think video games are a positive part of children's lives. Parents should help their children make smart choices when it comes to playing games. Then, children will get the most benefits from gaming.

Writer's Purpose: to explain the arguments for and against playing video games and to persuade the reader that there are benefits to playing video games

Page 138 / Student Book Page 99

Name: _____

Pro-Con Essay

Establishing Pros and Cons

Write a **pro** statement and a **con** statement for each topic.

1. **Topic:** students having cell phones in school

Pro	Con
Students can use them during an emergency.	Students face few emergencies that require a cell phone.

2. **Topic:** school lasting for the entire year

Pro	Con
Students would learn more.	Students and teachers would not get a break.

3. **Topic:** banning junk food at school

Pro	Con
Students and teachers will be healthier.	Having small treats occasionally can be part of a healthy diet.

4. **Topic:** making students learn cursive

Pro	Con
Students need to practice cursive to improve their handwriting.	Many people don't use cursive anymore because of computers.

Page 139 / Student Book Page 100

Name: _____   **Pro-Con Essay**

Writing an Introduction

Read each topic and the **pro** and **con** statements for that topic. Then write an introduction that grabs the readers' attention, clearly introduces the topic, and summarizes the pro and con positions on the topic.

1. **Topic:** drinking milk

   Pro: Milk has many vitamins and minerals that are good for people.

   Con: There are other foods that have the same vitamins and minerals as milk.

   A tall glass of cold milk can be refreshing, but is it healthy? People continue to argue over whether or not people should drink milk. Some think that milk is a nutritious part of a good diet, but with better food choices available, milk is an unnecessary drink.

2. **Topic:** limiting kids' time on the Internet

   Pro: Kids will be well-rounded if they spend less time on the Internet.

   Con: The Internet is an important part of a kid's academic and social life.

   Across the world, young people are clicking, tapping, browsing, and downloading. Kids today spend a lot of time online. It's true that the Internet is a very important part of a kid's school and social life. However, it is only one part of the many activities a young person should do in order to be happy and healthy.

© Evan-Moor Corp. • EMC 6015 • Nonfiction Writing   **PERSUASIVE WRITING**   139

Page 140 / Student Book Page 101

Name: _____   **Pro-Con Essay**

Adding Details and Examples

A. Check the box next to the sentence that provides the best detail or example for each **pro** and **con** statement.

1. **Pro statement:** Physical education, or P.E., helps students stay fit.
   - ☑ **Detail:** By going to P.E., students get the daily exercise they need.
   - ☐ **Detail:** All students love going to P.E. because they play games and run around.

2. **Con statement:** The school day should be used for academic subjects, not P.E.
   - ☐ **Detail:** Many students go home and play video games instead of exercising.
   - ☑ **Detail:** Students need time with a teacher in order to learn.

B. Read the topic and the *pro* and *con* statements. Write at least three details that tell more about each statement.

Topic: replacing textbooks with laptops

Pro statement: Laptop computers would make school easier for students.

Details: _Students can use a laptop to write, as well as read. Students who do not have access to a computer will be able to use the Internet. Students will learn useful computer skills while they learn about school subjects._

Con statement: Using laptops instead of textbooks creates many problems.

Details: _Computers break down frequently. Computers are more expensive than textbooks. Students will spend more time learning how to use computers instead of learning their subjects._

140 PERSUASIVE WRITING   Nonfiction Writing • EMC 6015 • © Evan-Moor Corp.

Lesson 3   Writing an Introduction

1. Say: **In a pro-con essay, your introduction should do three things: grab the readers' attention, introduce the topic or issue, and state your position.**

2. Group students and have each group read the introduction from the model on p. 137. Have groups identify the sentences that make the introduction interesting (*Boys in elementary ...; Are they wasting ...*), introduce the issue (*Are they wasting ...*), and give the writer's position (*While some people think ...*).

3. With the students still in groups, direct them to p. 139 and read the instructions aloud. Allow the groups to discuss the topics before they complete the activity. Consider moving among groups and helping students brainstorm ways to make the introduction interesting.

4. When students have finished, invite volunteers to share their introductions.

➤ **Extend the Lesson:** Have students write an introduction for one of the topics they brainstormed in the Lesson 1 extension activity. When students have finished, pair them and direct them to check their partner's introduction to make sure it is interesting, clearly introduces the topic, and states the writer's position.

Lesson 4   Adding Details and Examples

1. Say: **In a pro-con essay, you should include reasons and details for both sides of a topic or issue. This helps your reader learn more about the topic.**

2. Have students identify the details and examples in the writing model on p. 137. Suggest that students write *P* next to each detail that supports the *pro* argument (in favor of video games) and *C* next to each detail that supports the *con* argument (against video games). Point out that the details for each side of the argument are in separate paragraphs. Then say: **These details and examples clearly support and explain more about the pro and con statements.**

3. Direct students to p. 140 and read the instructions for Activity A aloud. Have students complete the activity, and then invite volunteers to share their answers and explain their thinking.

4. Read the instructions for Activity B aloud. Discuss the topic and the *pro* and *con* statements to make sure that students understand the issue. Then have them complete Activity B in pairs or small groups. Remind students that there are many details that can be added to support or explain the statements. Invite students to share their answers with the class.

➤ **Extend the Lesson:** Provide students with other *pro* and *con* statements. Have them independently write examples and details to elaborate on the statements.

Lesson 5 Balancing Pros and Cons

1. Explain that it is important to balance the *pro* and *con* details in a pro-con essay. Say: **You should have close to the same amount of information for the pro side of the argument as the con side. By doing so, you show your readers that you considered both sides of an issue before taking a stand on it.**

2. Have students decide if the *pro* and *con* details in "Is Gaming a Waste of Time?" are balanced. (yes–about the same amount of information on both sides) Say: **The amount of detail does not have to be exactly the same for both sides, but one side should not have much more detail than the other.**

3. Direct students to p. 141 and read the instructions aloud. Then group students and have them discuss each topic and make a list of details that could support both sides of the argument. After students have discussed the topics, have them complete the activity. Invite groups to share what they wrote.

➤ **Extend the Lesson:** Have students check that the details they listed in the Lesson 4 extension activity are balanced.

Lesson 6 Writing Conclusions

1. Say: **When you write a conclusion for a pro-con essay, you should clearly restate the topic or issue and your opinion about which side of the argument you agree with.**

2. Read aloud the conclusion from the writing model on p. 137. Ask volunteers to identify how it restates the issue (*While not everyone supports …*) and the writer's opinion (*Parents should help their children …*).

Page 141 / Student Book Page 102

Name: _____

Pro-Con Essay

Balancing Pros and Cons

Read the **pro** and **con** statements for each topic. Then think of details for each statement and write them in the space provided. Make sure the details for the **pro** statement are balanced against the details for the **con** statement.

1. **Topic:** keeping school open all year

   Pro: There are some good reasons to keep schools open year-round.
   Going to school in the summer will give students more time to learn what they need to know. And year-round schedules could also include more sports and other activities.

   Con: There are also good reasons why schools should close for the summer.
   Summer breaks give families time to take vacations and be together. And year-round school may not give students time to follow their own interests outside of school.

2. **Topic:** allowing vending machines in school

   Pro: Some parents think that vending machines don't belong in schools.
   They believe machines encourage students to waste their money and eat unhealthy foods. Students may choose to eat junk food instead of lunch.

   Con: Other people believe that vending machines have a place in schools. The cafeteria is not always open, and students get hungry throughout the day. And vending machines often have healthy snacks, such as granola bars and dried fruit.

© Evan-Moor Corp. • EMC 6015 • Nonfiction Writing   **PERSUASIVE WRITING** 141

Page 142 / Student Book Page 103

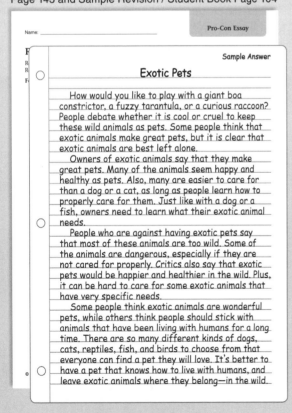

Name: _____

Pro-Con Essay

Writing Conclusions

For each topic, read the **pro** statement, the **con** statement, and the writer's opinion. Then write a conclusion that restates the topic and the writer's opinion.

1. **Topic:** setting aside a special area for dogs in the park
   Pro: Dogs and dog owners need a place outdoors to get exercise and bond. Parks already set aside places for picnics and playgrounds.
   Con: Dogs can be messy, loud, and poorly behaved. People who do not like dogs should not be forced to be around them.
   Writer's opinion: A special area for dogs in parks is a good idea.

   Not everyone agrees on whether parks should have special areas just for dogs. Dog owners want a place to play with their dogs and to meet other dog owners. But some park-goers do not like the noise from dogs or the bad behaviors of some dogs. However, if good rules were set up and followed, a special dog area in parks would be a good addition.

2. **Topic:** reducing the amount of violence in children's books
   Pro: With so much violence on television and in games, there is no need for it in children's books.
   Con: Children's books should not be censored.
   Writer's opinion: Books without violence are good additions to anyone's library.

   From video games to movies to books, violence is everywhere. But are the books that kids are reading too violent? Children's books often have less violence in them than many movies and almost all video games. However, this does not mean that books should describe acts of violence. Instead, it would be nice to see more books with less violence in them.

142 PERSUASIVE WRITING   Nonfiction Writing • EMC 6015 • © Evan-Moor Corp.

Page 143 and Sample Revision / Student Book Page 104

Name: _____

Pro-Con Essay

Sample Answer

Exotic Pets

How would you like to play with a giant boa constrictor, a fuzzy tarantula, or a curious raccoon? People debate whether it is cool or cruel to keep these wild animals as pets. Some people think that exotic animals make great pets, but it is clear that exotic animals are best left alone.

Owners of exotic animals say that they make great pets. Many of the animals seem happy and healthy as pets. Also, many are easier to care for than a dog or a cat, as long as people learn how to properly care for them. Just like with a dog or a fish, owners need to learn what their exotic animal needs.

People who are against having exotic pets say that most of these animals are too wild. Some of the animals are dangerous, especially if they are not cared for properly. Critics also say that exotic pets would be happier and healthier in the wild. Plus, it can be hard to care for some exotic animals that have very specific needs.

Some people think exotic animals are wonderful pets, while others think people should stick with animals that have been living with humans for a long time. There are so many different kinds of dogs, cats, reptiles, fish, and birds to choose from that everyone can find a pet they will love. It's better to have a pet that knows how to live with humans, and leave exotic animals where they belong—in the wild.

3. Direct students to p. 142 and complete number 1 as a class. Read aloud the topic, pro statement, con statement, and writer's opinion. Guide students through crafting a sentence that states the issue, summarizes the "pro" and "con" arguments, and incorporates the writer's opinion. Have students complete the activity in pairs. Ask volunteers to share their answers.

4. Have students complete number 2 independently or in pairs. Invite volunteers to read aloud their completed conclusions.

Lesson 7 Reviewing a Pro-Con Essay

1. Review the qualities of a good pro-con essay: an introduction that clearly introduces the issue and the writer's position, details elaborating on the *pro* and *con* arguments, balanced information, and a conclusion that restates the issue and the writer's opinion.

2. Have students read "Exotic Pets" on p. 143 independently, and then discuss what might be improved. For example, to help students elaborate on the cons of exotic pets, you may wish to have them brainstorm reasons against keeping exotic animals as pets. (e.g., Most exotic pets are not used to living in a home with people.) Also, tell students to correct any grammar, punctuation, and spelling errors in the draft.

3. Have students revise the essay independently on a separate sheet of paper. Remind them that there are different ways to fix the essay. Also remind them to proofread their revisions and check for errors.

4. Invite students to share their revisions with the class.

Name: _____

Introducing a Pro-Con Essay

Read this example of a good pro-con essay.

Writing Model

Is Gaming a Waste of Time?

Boys in elementary school spend an average of 13 hours every week playing video games. Girls spend an average of 5 hours gaming each week. Are they wasting their time? While some people think that video games are bad for children, the truth is that gamers learn valuable skills.

Many people worry about the harmful effects of playing video games. For example, some games have a lot of violence in them. And, unfortunately, some children do act more aggressive when they play violent video games. Also, children who spend too much time playing games often do worse in school than kids who do not spend as much time playing. And some adults worry that children who play video games do not get enough exercise.

Despite the concerns, children learn many positive skills when they play video games. Many games require players to solve problems, so players learn critical-thinking skills. And playing a game over and over teaches players to keep trying until they reach their goals. Playing video games also helps players improve their hand-eye coordination, which leads to a stronger brain. Finally, many new and popular video games require children to move around and exercise.

While not everyone supports video games, most parents think video games are a positive part of children's lives. Parents should help their children make smart choices when it comes to playing games. Then, children will get the most benefits from gaming.

Writer's Purpose: _____

_____

_____

Establishing Pros and Cons

Write a **pro** statement and a **con** statement for each topic.

1. **Topic:** students having cell phones in school

Pro	Con

2. **Topic:** school lasting for the entire year

Pro	Con

3. **Topic:** banning junk food at school

Pro	Con

4. **Topic:** making students learn cursive

Pro	Con

Writing an Introduction

Read each topic and the **pro** and **con** statements for that topic. Then write an introduction that grabs the readers' attention, clearly introduces the topic, and summarizes the pro and con positions on the topic.

1. **Topic:** drinking milk

    Pro: Milk has many vitamins and minerals that are good for people.

    Con: There are other foods that have the same vitamins and minerals as milk.

    _____

    _____

    _____

    _____

    _____

    _____

2. **Topic:** limiting kids' time on the Internet

    Pro: Kids will be well-rounded if they spend less time on the Internet.

    Con: The Internet is an important part of a kid's academic and social life.

    _____

    _____

    _____

    _____

    _____

    _____

Adding Details and Examples

A. Check the box next to the sentence that provides the best detail or example for each **pro** and **con** statement.

    1. **Pro statement:** Physical education, or P.E., helps students stay fit.

        ☐ **Detail:** By going to P.E., students get the daily exercise they need.

        ☐ **Detail:** All students love going to P.E. because they play games and run around.

    2. **Con statement:** The school day should be used for academic subjects, not P.E.

        ☐ **Detail:** Many students go home and play video games instead of exercising.

        ☐ **Detail:** Students need time with a teacher in order to learn.

B. Read the topic and the *pro* and *con* statements. Write at least three details that tell more about each statement.

Topic: replacing textbooks with laptops

Pro statement: Laptop computers would make school easier for students.

Details: _____

_____

_____

_____

Con statement: Using laptops instead of textbooks creates many problems.

Details: _____

_____

_____

_____

Name: _____

Balancing Pros and Cons

Read the **pro** and **con** statements for each topic. Then think of details for each statement and write them in the space provided. Make sure the details for the **pro** statement are balanced against the details for the **con** statement.

1. **Topic:** keeping school open all year

   Pro: There are some good reasons to keep schools open year-round.

   _____

   _____

   _____

   Con: There are also good reasons why schools should close for the summer.

   _____

   _____

   _____

2. **Topic:** allowing vending machines in school

   Pro: Some parents think that vending machines don't belong in schools.

   _____

   _____

   _____

   Con: Other people believe that vending machines have a place in schools.

   _____

   _____

   _____

Writing Conclusions

For each topic, read the **pro** statement, the **con** statement, and the writer's opinion. Then write a conclusion that restates the topic and the writer's opinion.

1. **Topic:** setting aside a special area for dogs in the park
   Pro: Dogs and dog owners need a place outdoors to get exercise and bond. Parks already set aside places for picnics and playgrounds.
   Con: Dogs can be messy, loud, and poorly behaved. People who do not like dogs should not be forced to be around them.
   Writer's opinion: A special area for dogs in parks is a good idea.

   _____

   _____

   _____

   _____

   _____

   _____

2. **Topic:** reducing the amount of violence in children's books
   Pro: With so much violence on television and in games, there is no need for it in children's books.
   Con: Children's books should not be censored.
   Writer's opinion: Books without violence are good additions to anyone's library.

   _____

   _____

   _____

   _____

   _____

   _____

Reviewing a Pro-Con Essay

Revise this essay. Use what you have learned to make it stronger.
Rewrite it on a separate sheet of paper.

Focus on:

✓ writing an introduction that introduces and sums up the *pro* and *con* main ideas

✓ writing clear *pro* and *con* statements

✓ adding details and examples to support the *pro* and *con* statements

✓ balancing the details for each side of the argument

✓ writing a conclusion that restates the issue and includes an opinion

✓ correcting grammar, punctuation, and spelling errors

Draft

Exotic Pets

Boa constrictors, tarantulas, and raccoons can be pets. There is much debate on weather it is cool or cruel to keep wild animals in a human house. Some people think that exotic animals make great pets.

Owners of exotic animals say that they make great pets. There are many reasons for this. They can easier to care for than some animals. Exotic animals is can be happy pets as long as people no how to take care of them. Owners, need to learn what their animal needs.

People who do not think exotic animals make good pets. They say most exotic pets are wild animals. They have other reasons, too.

There are enough kinds of animals to chose from for everyone to find a pet they will love. It's better to have a pet that knows how to live with people. Leaf exotic animals where they belongs—in the wild.

Writing a Personal Narrative

Page 147 / Student Book Page 106

Name: _____

Personal Narrative

Introducing a Personal Narrative
Read this example of a personal narrative.

Writing Model

Moving Day

It feels awful watching your best friend disappear. Vince Miller and I had been friends since kindergarten, but now the Millers were moving to Florida—more than a thousand miles away!

As I watched from my bedroom window, I saw the moving truck drive down our road. I felt as empty inside as the Miller's house. Then I smelled something sweet, my favorite snack! Mom had baked banana muffins to cheer me up. I ate one of the warm and buttery muffins, but it didn't help. Then I ate another to make sure. I still felt lousy, but at least I was lousy and full.

It was a beautiful day outside, hot and sunny. Normally, I'd be running around, and normally Vince would be there with me, too. I sighed and went into my room and started reading.

All of a sudden, I heard the squealing brakes of what sounded like a huge truck. Maybe the Millers had changed their mind and had come back! I raced downstairs and into the front yard.

But it wasn't them. A new family was already moving into the house. Two adults climbed out of the truck, along with a boy who looked about my age. The boy was carrying a plastic bag in both hands. He came over.

"Hi, I'm James," he said with a big smile. "And this is Bubbles, my goldfish. Do you have a bowl I can put him in?"

He told me he had ridden nine hours with the fish on his lap so that he could keep an eye on it. It was kind of neat that he cared about his fish so much, so I took James inside and found a bowl for Bubbles. We watched him swim for a while. Then I showed James the neighborhood.

When I got home, I ran upstairs and wrote Vince an e-mail about James and Bubbles. Then I ate one more banana muffin. The day turned out to be pretty good, after all.

Writer's Purpose: to tell what happened the day Vince
moved away

Page 148 / Student Book Page 107

Name: _____

Personal Narrative

Narrowing the Topic

For each broad topic, write a narrow topic. Then explain why the narrow topic is better.

Example

Broad topic: entering contests
Narrow topic: winning 3rd place at the science fair

The narrow topic is better because it tells about a specific contest when something exciting happened.

1. **Broad topic:** my best friend
   Narrow topic: the time we got stuck in a tree
   The narrow topic is better because it is about an afternoon that was scary and exciting

2. **Broad topic:** Thanksgiving
   Narrow topic: the time my dog ate the Thanksgiving turkey
   The narrow topic is better because it is about a funny and unique Thanksgiving

3. **Broad topic:** winter
   Narrow topic: building a snow dragon with my friend, Calen
   The narrow topic is better because it is about a specific time during winter when I made something with my friend

4. **Broad topic:** playing sports
   Narrow topic: scoring my first goal in a soccer game
   The narrow topic is better because it is about an exciting moment when something special happened to me

---

Lesson 1 Introducing a Personal Narrative

A personal narrative is writing that tells about a specific event or experience from the writer's life.

1. Ask students to recall a time when something memorable happened to them. Say: **When we write about one specific event in our lives, that is called a personal narrative. A personal narrative should make that event come alive for your readers.**

2. Have students read the model on p. 147. Then ask: **What is the purpose of this personal narrative?** (to tell what happened the day Vince moved away) Have students write the purpose on the lines provided.

3. Invite students to offer opinions about what makes this a good personal narrative. Prompt by asking: **Did the writer give details about one specific event? Did he write about what he saw, heard, and felt? Do the paragraphs flow easily from one to the next?**

➤ **Extend the Lesson:** Have students discuss why we tell each other stories about our own lives. Point out that sharing stories, especially about amusing or meaningful events, helps us understand each other. Discuss the similarities and differences between personal narratives, which tell true stories, and fiction, which tells made-up stories.

Lesson 2 Narrowing the Topic

1. Review the purpose of a personal narrative. Then say: **A good personal narrative focuses on one specific event. If you choose a topic that's too broad, you won't be able to tell a good story about it. So before you write, you need to choose a narrow topic.**

2. Remind students of the topic for "Moving Day" on p. 147. Then write the following on the board to show how the writer narrowed his topic before writing:

   Broad topic: my best friend Vince
   Narrow topic: the day Vince moved away

   Say: **The broad topic is just too much to write about. The narrow topic is better because it tells about one specific event that the writer remembers.**

3. Direct students to p. 148, read the instructions aloud, and guide students through the example. Point out that the explanation is specifically about the topic and not a generic response. Have students complete p. 148 independently. Invite volunteers to share their narrowed topics and their reasoning with the class.

Lesson 3 Using Sensory Details

1. Review the purpose of a personal narrative. Then say: **Using vivid details in a personal narrative helps your readers easily imagine the event you are writing about. Use details that appeal to the five senses.** Review the five senses and then say: **Sensory details help the reader feel that he or she is experiencing the event along with you.**

2. Have students identify the sensory details in "Moving Day." (*smelled something sweet, buttery, hot and sunny, squealing brakes,* etc.)

3. Have students complete Activity A on p. 149 in pairs. Encourage students to use details that appeal to each of the senses. Then have students share their responses with the class.

4. Model completing Activity B by writing this sentence on the board: *I heard the happy talk and laughter of people at the park.* Say: **Sentences like this tell your reader more than a sentence such as "I heard people talking."** The reader finds out more about the experience and understands how it felt. Have students complete the activity independently and share their sentences.

Lesson 4 Including Important Details

1. Review the purpose of a personal narrative. Then say: **A personal narrative should include details that are only about the topic or experience. To make your personal narratives stronger, remove details that are not about the topic or experience.**

2. Point out that all of the details in "Moving Day" on p. 147 are relevant. Then say: **You might think that details about eating the muffins aren't important, but they are. Why are those details relevant?** (e.g., They show how the writer felt after the Millers moved and reveal more about his personality.)

3. Direct students to p. 150 and guide them through the first item. Then have students complete the activity independently or in pairs. Ask volunteers to share their answers and explain their thinking.

Page 149 / Student Book Page 108

Name: _____   Personal Narrative

Using Sensory Details

A. For each topic, think of a personal experience and list at least three words or phrases that describe that experience. Try to list details that appeal to more than one sense.

1. **Topic:** a summer picnic

   Sensory details: green grass, bees buzzing, children laughing, sweet and sour lemonade, heat from sun, fried chicken

2. **Topic:** the first day of school this year

   Sensory details: kids in new clothes, woody scent of sharpened pencils, hard chair, teachers talking

B. Use the details you listed above to write a short descriptive paragraph about each topic.

1. **Topic:** a summer picnic

   The blazing heat from the sun warmed my skin. The bees were almost louder than the laughing children on the playground. I took a sip of tart lemonade and a bite of cold fried chicken.

2. **Topic:** the first day of school this year

   I rushed up the front steps, surrounded by laughter coming from the kids on all sides of me. By the sound of teachers calling names and the scent of sharpened pencils, I knew it was the start of a new school year.

© Evan-Moor Corp. • EMC 6015 • Nonfiction Writing   NARRATIVE WRITING 149

Page 150 / Student Book Page 109

Name: _____   Personal Narrative

Including Important Details

Cross out the sentences that do not belong in each paragraph.

1. After the storm, the beach was covered with trash. ~~Sometimes raccoons can get into trash cans and make a big mess.~~ We took a big garbage bag and went to pick things up. We found dozens of plastic bottles and metal cans. We even found a whole box of cereal. ~~My favorite cereal is Puff Pops.~~

2. While I was making a project for art class, my cat Bingo jumped up on the table. ~~Art class is my favorite class.~~ She knocked over the glitter and it went everywhere. ~~I hate it when I make a mess.~~ Then she started to walk all over my artwork. At first I was furious. But then I noticed that her red and gold footprints looked great on my painting.

3. When we got to the concert hall, there was a huge line out front. It wrapped all the way around the building. ~~The building had beautiful pillars and a lit dome.~~ I didn't want to wait, but Mom said we had no choice. So we started talking to the people in front of us. They had come from Texas. ~~That's the second largest state.~~ Talking with them made the wait go much faster.

4. The dentist's waiting room was very bright. The walls were painted light blue. I think the color was supposed to make me feel calm, but it didn't work. I felt pretty nervous. The last time I felt this nervous was when I gave a speech in class. ~~The speech was about Abraham Lincoln.~~ I wondered if I had any cavities. Would the dentist have to give me a shot? Would she use a drill? ~~My dentist's name is Dr. Harberger, but my brother calls her Dr. Hamburger.~~

5. Never let your mom's best friend cut your hair. Lita said she needed someone to practice on, so my mom volunteered me. ~~My mom makes me volunteer for everything. One time she made me clean up after a parade.~~ So I sat down in Lita's kitchen. There was no mirror, so I couldn't see what she was doing. Snip! Snip! Snip! The next thing I knew, half of my hair was on the floor.

6. Everyone from the neighborhood knew about Cruncher, the Doberman that lived at the end of Maple Street. ~~Many of the streets in our town are named after trees.~~ Cruncher loved crunching things in his jaws, especially new bicycles. As I rounded Maple Street on my shiny blue bike, my heart hammered in my chest. ~~It was a beautiful day outside.~~ I knew that Cruncher was waiting for me, dreaming about my tasty bicycle.

150 NARRATIVE WRITING   Nonfiction Writing • EMC 6015 • © Evan-Moor Corp.

© Evan-Moor Corp. • EMC 6015 • Nonfiction Writing   **NARRATIVE WRITING 145**

Page 151 / Student Book Page 110

Name: _____

Personal Narrative

Writing Transition Sentences

Read each short personal narrative. Add a transition sentence to connect the ideas in the two paragraphs.

1.   We waited and waited and waited in line for the new roller coaster at Action Park. There wasn't a scrap of shade anywhere, so we were incredibly hot. We crept forward a tiny bit every few minutes.

   <u>Finally, we got to the front of the line and hopped into our seats.</u>

Whoosh! In an instant, the coaster took off. It was worth the wait. What an amazing ride! We plunged down the height of a building and zoomed around a huge curve. Then we flipped upside down—three times!

2.   My sister knew exactly what she wanted to read. So when we got to the library, she walked right to the section about horses. She pulled the few books she had not read from the stacks and carried them to a comfy chair.

   <u>Unlike my sister, I never know what I want to read next.</u>

I wandered around, stopping here and there to read a few titles. The librarian saw me looking lost and asked me a few questions about the type of books I liked to read. Right away, she recommended several great books.

3.   The weather didn't look very promising for a picnic. Rain poured steadily all morning, and the sky was gray and dark. Dad thought we should go to the park anyway, but the rest of us weren't so sure.

   <u>However, when we got to the park, everything improved.</u>

The rain stopped and the sun came out. It didn't take much time for the grass to dry. We spread out the blanket, and Dad set up a delicious picnic. Sometimes it pays to be optimistic.

4.   Before the concert, I felt really nervous. I had never played the piano for anyone other than my family. I was hoping that there wouldn't be many people there. My knees began to wobble when I peeked from behind the curtain and saw the enormous crowd.

   <u>But as soon as I started playing, everything changed.</u>

My fingers knew what to do, and my legs stopped shaking. I played perfectly without even one mistake. By the end of the song, I had forgotten all about the audience. Then they started to clap, and I remembered where I was.

© Evan-Moor Corp. • EMC 6015 • Nonfiction Writing   **NARRATIVE WRITING**   151

Page 152 and Sample Revision / Student Book Page 111

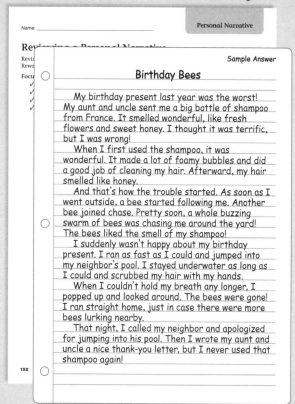

Name: _____

Personal Narrative

Sample Answer

Birthday Bees

   My birthday present last year was the worst! My aunt and uncle sent me a big bottle of shampoo from France. It smelled wonderful, like fresh flowers and sweet honey. I thought it was terrific, but I was wrong!
   When I first used the shampoo, it was wonderful. It made a lot of foamy bubbles and did a good job of cleaning my hair. Afterward, my hair smelled like honey.
   And that's how the trouble started. As soon as I went outside, a bee started following me. Another bee joined chase. Pretty soon, a whole buzzing swarm of bees was chasing me around the yard! The bees liked the smell of my shampoo!
   I suddenly wasn't happy about my birthday present. I ran as fast as I could and jumped into my neighbor's pool. I stayed underwater as long as I could and scrubbed my hair with my hands.
   When I couldn't hold my breath any longer, I popped up and looked around. The bees were gone! I ran straight home, just in case there were more bees lurking nearby.
   That night, I called my neighbor and apologized for jumping into his pool. Then I wrote my aunt and uncle a nice thank-you letter, but I never used that shampoo again!

152

---

1. Say: **When you write about an experience or event, you need to connect your ideas in a way that flows and helps the reader understand what happened. You need to write transition sentences, or sentences that guide your reader from one paragraph to the next in a way that makes sense.**

2. Direct students' attention to the first paragraph in "Moving Day" on p. 147. Point out that it introduces the topic: the writer's best friend moving away. Then remind students that the next paragraph tells how empty the writer felt about his friend moving away. Have a volunteer read aloud the first sentence of that paragraph. *(As I watched …)* Ask: **What does this sentence tell about?** (watching the moving truck leave) Say: **This sentence is a transition sentence. It connects the ideas in the two paragraphs.**

3. Have students work in groups to identify the other transition sentences in "Moving Day." *(It was a beautiful day …; But it wasn't them; "Hi, I'm James," he said …)* Say: **These transition sentences help the writing flow smoothly. They link the paragraphs together.**

4. Direct students to p. 151 and have them complete the activity. Explain that there is more than one way to write a good transition sentence. Ask volunteers to share their sentences.

Lesson 6 **Reviewing a Personal Narrative**

1. Review the qualities of a good personal narrative: a narrow topic, sensory details, relevant details, and transition sentences.

2. Have students read "Birthday Bees" on p. 152 and discuss what might be improved. For example, help them identify paragraphs that need transition sentences by reading the first two paragraphs aloud and pointing out that the ideas in the paragraphs are not connected. Also, remind students to correct grammar, punctuation, and spelling errors in the draft and to proofread and correct errors in their revisions.

3. Have students revise the personal narrative independently on a separate sheet of paper. Remind them that there may be different ways to improve the personal narrative.

4. Invite students to share their revisions with the class.

Name: _____

Introducing a Personal Narrative

Read this example of a personal narrative.

Writing Model

Moving Day

It feels awful watching your best friend disappear. Vince Miller and I had been friends since kindergarten, but now the Millers were moving to Florida—more than a thousand miles away!

As I watched from my bedroom window, I saw the moving truck drive down our road. I felt as empty inside as the Miller's house. Then I smelled something sweet, my favorite snack! Mom had baked banana muffins to cheer me up. I ate one of the warm and buttery muffins, but it didn't help. Then I ate another to make sure. I still felt lousy, but at least I was lousy and full.

It was a beautiful day outside, hot and sunny. Normally, I'd be running around, and normally Vince would be there with me, too. I sighed and went into my room and started reading.

All of a sudden, I heard the squealing brakes of what sounded like a huge truck. Maybe the Millers had changed their mind and had come back! I raced downstairs and into the front yard.

But it wasn't them. A new family was already moving into the house. Two adults climbed out of the truck, along with a boy who looked about my age. The boy was carrying a plastic bag in both hands. He came over.

"Hi, I'm James," he said with a big smile. "And this is Bubbles, my goldfish. Do you have a bowl I can put him in?"

He told me he had ridden nine hours with the fish on his lap so that he could keep an eye on it. It was kind of neat that he cared about his fish so much, so I took James inside and found a bowl for Bubbles. We watched him swim for a while. Then I showed James the neighborhood.

When I got home, I ran upstairs and wrote Vince an e-mail about James and Bubbles. Then I ate one more banana muffin. The day turned out to be pretty good, after all.

Writer's Purpose: _____

_____

Name: _____

Narrowing the Topic

For each broad topic, write a narrow topic. Then explain why the narrow topic is better.

> **Example**
>
> **Broad topic:** entering contests
> **Narrow topic:** winning 3rd place at the science fair
>
> <u>The narrow topic is better because it tells about a specific contest</u>
> <u>when something exciting happened.</u>

1. **Broad topic:** my best friend

   Narrow topic: _____

   The narrow topic is better because _____

   _____.

2. **Broad topic:** Thanksgiving

   Narrow topic: _____

   The narrow topic is better because _____

   _____.

3. **Broad topic:** winter

   Narrow topic: _____

   The narrow topic is better because _____

   _____.

4. **Broad topic:** playing sports

   Narrow topic: _____

   The narrow topic is better because _____

   _____.

Using Sensory Details

A. For each topic, think of a personal experience and list at least three words or phrases that describe that experience. Try to list details that appeal to more than one sense.

   1. **Topic:** a summer picnic

      Sensory details: _____

      _____

   2. **Topic:** the first day of school this year

      Sensory details: _____

      _____

B. Use the details you listed above to write a short descriptive paragraph about each topic.

   1. **Topic:** a summer picnic

      _____

      _____

      _____

      _____

   2. **Topic:** the first day of school this year

      _____

      _____

      _____

      _____

Including Important Details

Cross out the sentences that do not belong in each paragraph.

1. After the storm, the beach was covered with trash. Sometimes raccoons can get into trash cans and make a big mess. We took a big garbage bag and went to pick things up. We found dozens of plastic bottles and metal cans. We even found a whole box of cereal. My favorite cereal is Puff Pops.

2. While I was making a project for art class, my cat Bingo jumped up on the table. Art class is my favorite class. She knocked over the glitter and it went everywhere. I hate it when I make a mess. Then she started to walk all over my artwork. At first I was furious. But then I noticed that her red and gold footprints looked great on my painting.

3. When we got to the concert hall, there was a huge line out front. It wrapped all the way around the building. The building had beautiful pillars and a lit dome. I didn't want to wait, but Mom said we had no choice. So we started talking to the people in front of us. They had come from Texas. That's the second largest state. Talking with them made the wait go much faster.

4. The dentist's waiting room was very bright. The walls were painted light blue. I think the color was supposed to make me feel calm, but it didn't work. I felt pretty nervous. The last time I felt this nervous was when I gave a speech in class. The speech was about Abraham Lincoln. I wondered if I had any cavities. Would the dentist have to give me a shot? Would she use a drill? My dentist's name is Dr. Harberger, but my brother calls her Dr. Hamburger.

5. Never let your mom's best friend cut your hair. Lita said she needed someone to practice on, so my mom volunteered me. My mom makes me volunteer for everything. One time she made me clean up after a parade. So I sat down in Lita's kitchen. There was no mirror, so I couldn't see what she was doing. Snip! Snip! Snip! The next thing I knew, half of my hair was on the floor.

6. Everyone from the neighborhood knew about Cruncher, the Doberman that lived at the end of Maple Street. Many of the streets in our town are named after trees. Cruncher loved crunching things in his jaws, especially new bicycles. As I rounded Maple Street on my shiny blue bike, my heart hammered in my chest. It was a beautiful day outside. I knew that Cruncher was waiting for me, dreaming about my tasty bicycle.

Writing Transition Sentences

Read each short personal narrative. Add a transition sentence to connect the ideas in the two paragraphs.

1. We waited and waited and waited in line for the new roller coaster at Action Park. There wasn't a scrap of shade anywhere, so we were incredibly hot. We crept forward a tiny bit every few minutes.

   _____

   Whoosh! In an instant, the coaster took off. It was worth the wait. What an amazing ride! We plunged down the height of a building and zoomed around a huge curve. Then we flipped upside down—three times!

2. My sister knew exactly what she wanted to read. So when we got to the library, she walked right to the section about horses. She pulled the few books she had not read from the stacks and carried them to a comfy chair.

   _____

   I wandered around, stopping here and there to read a few titles. The librarian saw me looking lost and asked me a few questions about the type of books I liked to read. Right away, she recommended several great books.

3. The weather didn't look very promising for a picnic. Rain poured steadily all morning, and the sky was gray and dark. Dad thought we should go to the park anyway, but the rest of us weren't so sure.

   _____

   The rain stopped and the sun came out. It didn't take much time for the grass to dry. We spread out the blanket, and Dad set up a delicious picnic. Sometimes it pays to be optimistic.

4. Before the concert, I felt really nervous. I had never played the piano for anyone other than my family. I was hoping that there wouldn't be many people there. My knees began to wobble when I peeked from behind the curtain and saw the enormous crowd.

   _____

   My fingers knew what to do, and my legs stopped shaking. I played perfectly without even one mistake. By the end of the song, I had forgotten all about the audience. Then they started to clap, and I remembered where I was.

Reviewing a Personal Narrative

Revise this personal narrative. Use what you have learned to make it stronger.
Rewrite it on a separate sheet of paper.

Focus on:

✓ using sensory details to describe the event
✓ including only details that are about the topic
✓ writing transition sentences to connect paragraphs
✓ correcting grammar, punctuation, and spelling errors

Draft

Birthday Bees

I gots the worst birthday present ever last year. At first, I thought it was great. My aunt and uncle sended me a package. From their trip to France. They live in Detroit. It was a big bottle of shampoo. It smelled good, like flowers and honey. Last year, they gave me a book about mummies for my birthday.

The shampoo made a lot of bubble's and did a great job cleaning my hair. Afterward, my hair smelled.

As soon as I went outside, a bee starts to follow me. Then another bee, joined the chase and another bee joins after that, too! Pretty soon, a whole swarm was chasing me around the yard. The bees liked the smell of my shampoo! Bees gather nectar from flowers and use it to make honey.

I ran and jumped into my neighbor's pool. I stayed underwater as long as I could, and I scrubbed my hair with my hands.

I quickly looked around. The bees were gone! I ran straight home, just in case there was more bees lurking nearby.

That night, I called my naybor and apolijized for jumping into his pool. Then I wrote my aunt and uncle a nice thank-you letter, but I never used that shampoo again!

Writing Creative Nonfiction

Lesson 1 Introducing Creative Nonfiction

Creative nonfiction is narrative writing that tells a true story by using elements of creative writing.

1. Say: **Creative nonfiction is a special form of nonfiction writing. It tells about something that really happened, but it is written like a story.**

2. Have students read the model on p. 156. Ask students to identify the purpose. (to tell a true story about good sportsmanship) Have students write the purpose on the lines provided.

3. Invite students to offer opinions about what makes this good creative nonfiction. Prompt by asking questions such as: **Does the first paragraph sound more like a story than a report? Does the writer use strong verbs and vivid language? What feeling or mood did the writer create?** Then explain that students will use the model as they study the skills needed to write good creative nonfiction.

➤ **Extend the Lesson:** Have students read other examples of creative nonfiction from magazines or textbooks. If possible, have students read a piece of creative nonfiction and an expository report on the same topic to understand the differences between the forms.

Lesson 2 Writing a Creative Introduction

1. Say: **In creative nonfiction, the introduction should introduce the topic in an interesting way so that your readers want to continue reading.** Have a volunteer read aloud the introduction in "True Sportsmanship." Ask: **Which sentence introduces the topic?** *(When the women's softball teams from Central Washington University and Western Oregon University met to play …)* Then ask: **How does the writer make the introduction interesting?** (by building suspense, writing that the game would be the most talked about game, etc.)

2. Direct students to p. 157 and read the directions aloud. Then say: **There are many ways to make an introduction interesting or creative. The writer of "True Sportsmanship" used suspense. You can also surprise your reader or give a vivid description of your subject.** Read aloud the example and discuss with students what makes the revised introduction more interesting. (used suspense to talk about the storm, vividly described what the storm looked like, and so on)

Page 156 / Student Book Page 113

Name: _____

Creative Nonfiction

Introducing Creative Nonfiction

Read this example of creative nonfiction.

Writing Model

True Sportsmanship

When the women's softball teams from Central Washington University and Western Oregon University met to play on April 28, 2008, they had no idea that it would become the most talked about game in the country. By the second inning, neither team had scored, but Western Oregon had two runners on base. Then right fielder Sara Tucholsky stepped up to bat.

The first pitch rocketed past as Sara swung and missed. A few hecklers in the crowd yelled to break her intense concentration, but she ignored them. She was determined to hit the ball. She swung hard at the next pitch. The ball smacked sharply against the bat and sailed away.

Sara had just hit her first home run in four years! She flashed a smile as wide as the Grand Canyon and began jogging around the bases. But she was so excited that she ran past first base without touching it. She realized that the play would not count unless she touched the base, so she turned back. Then disaster struck.

As Sara turned her body around, she tore a ligament in her knee. Sara screamed in pain and crumpled to the ground. She crawled to first base, but there was no way she could complete her run around the other bases. According to the rules, this meant she would not score.

Sara's coach did not know what to do. She did not want Sara to lose her home run, and the umpire said that Sara's teammates were not allowed to help her. But then, something amazing happened. Two young women from the other team, Mallory Holtman and Liz Wallace, ran over to Sara and carefully picked her up. They carried her around the bases, stopping by each base and gently lowering Sara so that she could touch the base with her foot.

When the three reached home plate, Sara's teammates were in tears. The crowd cheered wildly. With help from Mallory and Liz, Sara completed a home run. In the end, Western Oregon won the game, but the score is not what people remember about that day.

News of the young women's incredible act of sportsmanship traveled around the world. Later that year, Sara, Mallory, and Liz won the 2008 ESPY award for the year's "Best Moment" in sports.

Writer's Purpose: to tell a true story about good sportsmanship

Nonfiction Writing • EMC 6015 • © Evan-Moor Corp.

Page 157 / Student Book Page 114

Name: _____

Creative Nonfiction

Writing a Creative Introduction

Read the following introductions to two true stories. Revise each introduction to introduce the topic in a more interesting way.

Example

On April 14, 1935, a dust storm hit Stratford, Texas. The storm struck on a Sunday. People were busy in town or at church. The storm lasted for four hours. Everything was covered in dust. People were scared.

April 14, 1935 began as a normal Sunday for people in Stratford, Texas. People were busy in town or sitting in church. Nobody realized that a terrible dust storm would soon attack and blanket everything in dust for hours.

1. Gander was a dog who lived with Canadian soldiers during World War II. In 1941, the soldiers went to Hong Kong Island, and they took Gander with them. Canada was at war with Japan. One night, Japanese soldiers came to attack the Canadian soldiers, but Gander heard the Japanese soldiers coming. He barked and warned the Canadian soldiers. This saved their lives.

In 1941, Gander traveled with Canadian soldiers to Hong Kong. One night, he heard Japanese soldiers sneaking toward the camp, and he warned the others. The Canadian soldiers were saved! Gander was a hero—and a dog!

2. Erik Weihenmayer was born blind. In 2001, Erik became the first blind person to climb Mount Everest, the world's tallest mountain. It is difficult for most people to climb. The wind is cold and icy, and there are many storms. Erik struggled, but he kept going until he reached the top on May 25, 2011.

Erik Weihenmayer did not let being blind stop him from having a big adventure. In 2001, Erik climbed the world's tallest mountain, Mount Everest. Erik struggled through the icy storms, but he never gave up. On May 25, 2001, Erik made it to the highest point on Earth.

© Evan-Moor Corp. • EMC 6015 • Nonfiction Writing   **NARRATIVE WRITING   157**

Writing Creative Nonfiction, continued

Page 158 / Student Book Page 115

Name: _____

Creative Nonfiction

Including Strong Verbs, Adjectives, and Adverbs

Revise each description. Replace weak verbs with strong ones, and add adjectives and adverbs to create better, more creative descriptions.

1. The sisters made a fort in their yard. Then they added furniture.

   The clever sisters constructed a massive cardboard fort in their tiny yard. Then they decorated inside with brightly painted plastic furniture.

2. Sunlight came into the room through the curtains. A dog was asleep on the floor. Then a noise made the dog get up.

   Bright, golden sunlight trickled into the room through lacy curtains. A large black dog snored loudly on the floor. Then a sudden noise startled the dog out of its sleep.

3. The soccer team was at the tournament. They beat the other team. The players were happy during the ride home.

   The soccer team trounced the other team in the thrilling tournament. The excited players cheered and laughed often during the ride home.

4. Petra closed the door, got her backpack, and went upstairs to her room. She sat on her bed and got a novel.

   Petra carefully shut the front door, lifted her heavy backpack, and tiptoed upstairs to her tiny room. Then she silently climbed onto her bed and began reading a mystery novel.

158 NARRATIVE WRITING   Nonfiction Writing • EMC 6015 • © Evan-Moor Corp.

---

3. Guide students through the activity, helping them brainstorm ways that each introduction could be improved.

Lesson 3 Including Strong Verbs, Adjectives, and Adverbs

1. Say: **Strong verbs create more interesting and descriptive sentences.** Write the following sentences on the board: *Maria ate her lunch. Maria devoured her lunch.* Ask: **How does *devoured* tell us more about Maria and her lunch?** (She ate quickly, she was hungry, etc.) Have students underline the strong verbs in "True Sportsmanship." (e.g., *rocketed, smacked, sailed, flashed, tore, crumpled, screamed, crawled*)

2. Say: **Good writers also use specific adjectives and adverbs to describe.** Write the following sentences on the board: *The movie was good. The movie was hilarious and exciting.* Ask: **How do *hilarious* and *exciting* tell us more about the movie than *good* does?** (They are more specific and clearer, they tell how or why the movie was good, etc.) Have students circle specific adjectives and adverbs in the model. (*intense, sharply, amazing, vividly, incredible, gently,* etc.)

3. Direct students to p. 158 and read the directions aloud. If necessary, complete the first item as a class. Then have students complete the activity independently or in small groups.

4. Invite volunteers to read aloud their revisions and have listeners identify the strong verbs, adjectives, and adverbs the writer used.

➤ **Extend the Lesson:** Have students create word webs to think of strong verbs that can replace common verbs such as *run, walk, go, eat, have, like,* and *make.*

Lesson 4 Creating a Mood

1. Say: **Mood is the feeling that a piece of writing gives you as you read it. You can create a particular mood with your choice of words. You can choose words that create many moods, such as exciting, suspenseful, scary, sad, thrilling, cheerful, or mysterious moods.**

2. Revisit "True Sportsmanship" and ask: **What kind of mood did the writer create?** (e.g., suspenseful) **Which words or phrases helped create this mood?** (*Then disaster struck; Sarah's coach did not know what to do;* etc.)

3. Write this sentence on the board: *The boy rode his bike.* Ask: **How can we revise this sentence to create a scarier mood?** (e.g., The terrified boy slowly rode his bike up the dark lane toward the haunted house.) **How can we make it funny?** (e.g., The tall teenage boy awkwardly pedaled his little sister's pink, sparkly bike.)

4. Have students complete the activity on p. 159 independently or in pairs. Then have volunteers read aloud their revisions and ask listeners to identify the details that helped create the assigned mood.

➤ **Extend the Lesson:** Have students brainstorm lists of adjectives that can be used to describe different moods. (e.g., **spooky:** *dark, stormy, loud, chilling, ghostly*)

Lesson 5 Reviewing Creative Nonfiction

1. Review the qualities of good creative nonfiction: a creative introduction; strong verbs, adjectives, and adverbs; and a specific mood.

2. Explain that students are going to read about a kayaker named Pedro Olivia, who was trying to break a world record. If possible, show them pictures and/or videos of people kayaking or of Pedro Olivia's plunge.

3. Have students read "The Longest Plunge" on p. 160 and discuss what might be improved. Explain that while there is technically nothing wrong with the essay, it is not very creative. Help them determine possible moods, such as suspenseful or thrilling, and where they could change details or add sentences to create that mood. (e.g., in paragraphs 2 and 3) Suggest that students imagine how Pedro felt that day.

4. Have students revise the essay independently on a separate sheet of paper. Remind students that creative nonfiction tells a true story, so they should not change any of the facts in the essay. Their revisions should simply tell the same story in a more creative way.

5. Invite students to share their revisions with the class. Remind them that there may be different ways to improve the creative nonfiction essay.

Page 159 / Student Book Page 116

Name: _____

Creative Nonfiction

Creating a Mood

Revise each description. Add details and use descriptive words to create the mood given in parentheses.

1. The package came in the mail. Keith opened it. He smiled. **(exciting)**

   At last, the package Keith had been waiting for finally arrived! Keith ripped open the box. His eyes lit up, and he grinned from ear to ear.

2. It was a rainy day. Lakshmi sat and stared out the window. **(gloomy)**

   The sky was cloudy and gray. Lakshmi sighed as she watched little streams of rain drizzle slowly down the window.

3. Trey looked inside the room. Two eyes were watching him. **(scary)**

   Trey peeked nervously into the dark room. Large yellow eyes glared at him from the corner. His heart started to pound.

4. Duke looked at his coach. Then he turned around and walked away. **(angry)**

   Duke glared angrily at his coach. Then he turned his back on the coach and stomped away.

5. Lacey lost her new bracelet. She looked everywhere for it. **(mysterious)**

   Lacey knew she had put on her bracelet this morning. But now it was nowhere to be found. She had searched every room in the school twice. Where could it have gone?

© Evan-Moor Corp. • EMC 6015 • Nonfiction Writing   **NARRATIVE WRITING** 159

Page 160 and Sample Revision / Student Book Page 117

Name: _____

Creative Nonfiction

Sample Answer

The Longest Plunge

On March 4, 2009, Pedro Olivia spent the morning carefully preparing himself at the Salto Belo waterfall in Brazil. He studied the 127-foot-tall waterfall, looking for the safest route. He was determined to set a world record for the highest waterfall plunge in a kayak.

When Pedro felt sure he could safely take the plunge, he strapped on his helmet and climbed into his kayak. He cautiously paddled toward the fall's edge.

The current quickly sped Pedro on his way. His heart pounded as his kayak drew closer and closer to the edge. Time stood still as the front of his kayak bobbed over the drop-off. Then he fell. Pedro's fall lasted for three seconds, but it seemed like forever. During the fall, his kayak flipped upside down, so Pedro landed headfirst in the water. However, the landing was successful. He had picked a good spot in the falls to hit the water.

Pedro stayed underwater for five long seconds. When he came up to the surface, he was still in his kayak. Pedro had broken the world record!

But Pedro's journey wasn't quite finished. He was now stuck behind the waterfall and had to climb out of his boat. That's when he noticed the snakes! Several boa constrictors were lying on the rocks. Slipping and sliding, he climbed out from behind the waterfall. Pedro Olivia had just survived the longest descent ever made in a kayak.

© Evan-Moor Corp. • EMC 6015 • Nonfiction Writing   **NARRATIVE WRITING** 155

Name: _____

Introducing Creative Nonfiction

Read this example of creative nonfiction.

Writing Model

True Sportsmanship

When the women's softball teams from Central Washington University and Western Oregon University met to play on April 28, 2008, they had no idea that it would become the most talked about game in the country. By the second inning, neither team had scored, but Western Oregon had two runners on base. Then right fielder Sara Tucholsky stepped up to bat.

The first pitch rocketed past as Sara swung and missed. A few hecklers in the crowd yelled to break her intense concentration, but she ignored them. She was determined to hit the ball. She swung hard at the next pitch. The ball smacked sharply against the bat and sailed away.

Sara had just hit her first home run in four years! She flashed a smile as wide as the Grand Canyon and began jogging around the bases. But she was so excited that she ran past first base without touching it. She realized that the play would not count unless she touched the base, so she turned back. Then disaster struck.

As Sara turned her body around, she tore a ligament in her knee. Sara screamed in pain and crumpled to the ground. She crawled to first base, but there was no way she could complete her run around the other bases. According to the rules, this meant she would not score.

Sara's coach did not know what to do. She did not want Sara to lose her home run, and the umpire said that Sara's teammates were not allowed to help her. But then, something amazing happened. Two young women from the other team, Mallory Holtman and Liz Wallace, ran over to Sara and carefully picked her up. They carried her around the bases, stopping by each base and gently lowering Sara so that she could touch the base with her foot.

When the three reached home plate, Sara's teammates were in tears. The crowd cheered wildly. With help from Mallory and Liz, Sara completed a home run. In the end, Western Oregon won the game, but the score is not what people remember about that day.

News of the young women's incredible act of sportsmanship traveled around the world. Later that year, Sara, Mallory, and Liz won the 2008 ESPY award for the year's "Best Moment" in sports.

Writer's Purpose: _____

Name: _____

Writing a Creative Introduction

Read the following introductions to two true stories. Revise each introduction to introduce the topic in a more interesting way.

On April 14, 1935, a dust storm hit Stratford, Texas. The storm struck on a Sunday. People were busy in town or at church. The storm lasted for four hours. Everything was covered in dust. People were scared.

April 14, 1935 began as a normal Sunday for people in Stratford, Texas. People were busy in town or sitting in church. Nobody realized that a terrible dust storm would soon attack and blanket everything in dust for hours.

1.   Gander was a dog who lived with Canadian soldiers during World War II. In 1941, the soldiers went to Hong Kong Island, and they took Gander with them. Canada was at war with Japan. One night, Japanese soldiers came to attack the Canadian soldiers, but Gander heard the Japanese soldiers coming. He barked and warned the Canadian soldiers. This saved their lives.

_____

_____

_____

_____

2.   Erik Weihenmayer was born blind. In 2001, Erik became the first blind person to climb Mount Everest, the world's tallest mountain. It is difficult for most people to climb. The wind is cold and icy, and there are many storms. Erik struggled, but he kept going until he reached the top on May 25, 2011.

_____

_____

_____

_____

Including Strong Verbs, Adjectives, and Adverbs

Revise each description. Replace weak verbs with strong ones, and add adjectives and adverbs to create better, more creative descriptions.

1. The sisters made a fort in their yard. Then they added furniture.

   _____

   _____

   _____

2. Sunlight came into the room through the curtains. A dog was asleep on the floor. Then a noise made the dog get up.

   _____

   _____

   _____

3. The soccer team was at the tournament. They beat the other team. The players were happy during the ride home.

   _____

   _____

   _____

4. Petra closed the door, got her backpack, and went upstairs to her room. She sat on her bed and got a novel.

   _____

   _____

   _____

   _____

Name: _____

Creating a Mood

Revise each description. Add details and use descriptive words to create the mood given in parentheses.

1. The package came in the mail. Keith opened it. He smiled. **(exciting)**

    _____

    _____

    _____

2. It was a rainy day. Lakshmi sat and stared out the window. **(gloomy)**

    _____

    _____

    _____

3. Trey looked inside the room. Two eyes were watching him. **(scary)**

    _____

    _____

    _____

4. Duke looked at his coach. Then he turned around and walked away. **(angry)**

    _____

    _____

    _____

5. Lacey lost her new bracelet. She looked everywhere for it. **(mysterious)**

    _____

    _____

    _____

Name: _____

Reviewing Creative Nonfiction

Revise this creative nonfiction piece. Use what you have learned to make it stronger. Rewrite it on a separate sheet of paper.

Focus on:

✓ writing a creative introduction
✓ including strong verbs, adjectives, and adverbs
✓ creating a mood
✓ correcting grammar, punctuation, and spelling errors

Draft

The Longest Plunge

On March 4, 2009, Pedro Olivia went to the Salto Belo waterfall in Brazil. It were 127 feet tall. He looked at the waterfall. He wanted a safe route down. He was going to set a world record for the highest waterfall plunge in a kayak.

Pedro put on his helmit and got into his kayak. He moved toward the fall's. The curent is taking him to the edge of the falls. Time stood still as the front of his kayak bobbed in the air over the edge. Then his kayak went down.

Pedro fell at 70 miles per hour. His kayak flips over, and he landed headfirst in the water. The landing was not bad. He had picked a good spot in the falls to hit the water.

Pedro remained underwater. For five seconds. He came to the surface, still in his kayak. This meant he had broken the record.

Pedro's experiense was not over. He was stuck in a pool behind the waterfall. He climbed out of the boat and saw several snakes on the rock's. They were long boa constrictors. Pedro walked around them and goes back to shore.